CRITICAL

BEGINNER'S GUIDE:

LEARN HOW REASONING BY LOGIC IMPROVES EFFECTIVE PROBLEM SOLVING. THE TOOLS TO THINK SMARTER, LEVEL UP INTUITION TO REACH YOUR POTENTIAL AND GROW YOUR MINDFULNESS.

Please consult a licensed professional before attempting any techniques outlined in this book.

By reading this document, the reader agrees that under no circumstances is the author responsible for any losses, direct or indirect, which are incurred as a result of the use of information contained within this document, including, but not limited to, — errors, omissions, or inaccuracies.

Table of Contents

Introduction

Many of us haven't reached our full potential. We can be someone. But oftentimes, we think that we cannot. This is the main reason which hinders our success. That thought is a big lie. We are highly capable and we were designed to have the capability to shape our destiny. However, the superb potential that lies within remains dormant and untapped. It is mostly undeveloped. That is why we need to train and improve our thinking. Humans have the unique gift to be able to learn anything they want. The best way to improve our thinking is to train. It is the same training to improve in sports, dancing or playing musical instruments, only with a different method. It requires patience and hard work. Such improvement will only take place with willingness, commitment, and dedication to learn. On the other hand, we will reap painful consequences if we do not take this seriously. This development we desire is a process that requires a lot of work. No matter the will, it is impossible to become a critical thinker overnight. It is a challenging, long-term process. It might even take a couple of years just to change our thinking habits. The ideal and vital characteristics of a true critical thinker require an even longer period to attain full development. How can we train our minds? How can critical thinking be attained? How can we apply critical thinking on a daily basis? How can we fuel our minds and reach our full potential to live the life we desire?

Accept

Yes, we need to accept that problems lie in our thinking. It is a need to say yes to the challenge in improving our thinking. Most people who begin the challenge are unaware of significant problems in our thinking. They are unreflective thinkers. Hence, we need to get out of this stage. Sometimes our ego and pride hinder us from committing to learning; we likewise need to get rid of these to begin a regular practice. So, ask yourself over and over again, do you fully accept that you were once an unreflective thinker? If you consistently answer yes, then you are ready.

Start accepting yourself with the following tips:

Above all, accept yourself without hatred.

Use non-blaming and simple phrases. In your case, say "I am an unreflective thinker".

Assess yourself without blaming and self-hate. Blaming only leads to being defensive, which will bring out your ego and pride.

Perform relaxation breathing if you begin feeling defensive and self-hating.

Affirmative statements as you embark towards change will always help.

A good laugh will make acceptance of your weakness, which is unreflective thinking, easier.

Remember that improving critical thinking is a part of your personal growth. You must accept yourself and your weakness to give way to a better you.

Evaluate Your Thinking

Evaluate your weaknesses and strengths in thinking. The following are questions you might ask yourself.

What was on my mind today? Did negative thoughts disturb me today?

Did I figure anything out today?

When did I do my best thinking today?

When did I do my worst?

Have I done something beneficial to my goals today?

If I had a chance to repeat the day, what would I do differently? Why?

If every day was lived in this manner for a year, will something be accomplished at the end of the year?

Now, evaluate yourself. Of course, it is necessary to ponder and reflect upon the questions. You are now a challenged thinker, aware of your problems in thinking. Your pattern of thinking will be noticeable in the soonest time.

Make the Most of Your Time

We all waste some time. Applying time management tactics seems to be hard work for all of us. We do not use the whole of our time in a productive manner. We even skip one activity to prioritize another in some instances. We realize later that none of them was enjoyed. We even get easily frustrated and irritated with small matters or matters we could never control. We do not plan well, and our poor planning yields us regrets and consequences. We end up with problems that could have been heeded, solved, and avoided.

Here is an example. If we left earlier to get to our destination, the long hours we suffer in a traffic jam could have been avoided. We even waste time over thinking of our regrets in the past. Or we just blankly stare off into space sometimes.

Time is irreversible. It is gone. We should have spent it well and carefully examined our options.

In that way, we would never have wasted any of it. So next time, why not take advantage of the time you normally waste by improving your critical thinking?

Maximize your time for critical thinking through the following:

1. Read an interesting book or feature when you're feeling idle.

2. Write down your thoughts about different topics.

3. Test your brain regularly through quizzes or puzzles.

4. Practice freethinking or logic-based thinking as you read.

Avoid being idle by maximizing your time spent on improving critical thinking. Challenge and train your thinking whenever you have spare time and start building your foundation towards being a critical thinker.

Chapter 1

What Is Critical Thinking?

Define Target. Critical Thinking – The objective analysis and evaluation of an issue in order to form a judgment.

The key part of that definition is in order to form a judgment. Critical Thinking comes BEFORE the judgment.

Do you notice how much more common it is to see people's judgments come first? People work very hard to believe what they want to believe. And that's stupid. It makes for some very entertaining stories though.

Nothing is more amusing than watching someone working hard to make their wrong answer be the right one. Remember when Ahmadinejad claimed there were no gay people in Iran? Still one of our favorites... not exactly a critical thinker there.

Or how about all the people who branded Galileo a heretic for proving the earth revolved around the sun. It is far easier to convince people they're at the center of the universe. I'll bet we could still convince a fair percentage of people Galileo was wrong, even today. But life is already difficult enough for stupid people. You can argue all night that the sun isn't coming up in the morning, and it will still rise and prove you wrong. It would have been much better to get a good night's sleep. Life is like that. You can think whatever you want and probably muddle through, but it's easier if you use the right answers.

A critical thinker has an easier life. They think about the questions before deciding on their answers. The right answer is a lot easier to accept when it finally shows up if you haven't already made a decision. The amount of energy stupid people waste trying to defend their wrong answers could be used to make their lives better. Instead, they waste it trying to make their wrong answer right.

Critical thinking is a method for dealing with the information overload we have today. You just let the data come in and apply critical thinking principles to determine its value. Most information is worthless and you will quickly reject it. It becomes automatic too. It wastes your time and that might even make you a little angry. Which is good because it helps you reject it faster next time.

Some information will be valuable. We need a little, a very small fraction of what is thrown at us every day, but we do need some. Gathering enough valuable information will take you to the answers you need. After you have what you need, the rest is rejected.

Once you know HOW to think, the rest is just plugging in the data. You pick the question, apply some critical thinking principles, and a short time later you have an answer that makes your life better.

Chapter 2

Core Critical Thinking Skills

Critical thinking itself is made up of several different skill sets that come together and allow you to interpret and understand the information you are attempting to analyze in the first place. These critical thinking skills are largely important to you in several different contexts, even if they may not necessarily seem important upfront. When you develop these critical thinking skills, you are ensuring that you are capable of managing nearly any situation that requires you to think and problem solve. When you are able to make judgments that are both purposeful and reflective, you are going to find that you are far more capable of handling anything that life throws at you.

Interpretation

The first of the important skills that you must master to think critically is interpretation. When you are able to interpret, you can comprehend and also communicate the significance of whatever it is that you are discussing. Consider that you are looking at that problem with your children again—they are all crying for help, and you need to figure out what to do with them. When you are able to interpret the situation around you, you are gathering information about what is around you and starting to figure out what is happening. In being able to interpret, you are able to recognize the significance of your experiences—this means that you can compare the children crying around you to the instances in which they cried before. You can recognize that your oldest child tends to only cry when there is something wrong, while the baby usually cries whenever anything is wrong, and so on. You are able to understand what is happening around you, thanks to your past experiences, situations, judgments, beliefs, or other instances that may be relevant.

When you are using interpretation, there are several other categories of subskills that are relevant: these subskills are necessary in order to ensure that you are capable of truly understanding what you hope to interpret. These subskills include:

Categorization: You can sort the event that you are currently experiencing or observing into categories with similar events in the past. For example, you are able to lump in your infant crying with the other times that your infant has cried for food.

Decoding significance: You can figure out which events are significant versus insignificant or not worth attention. When you are looking over your child crying over the television that needs to be on, you are able to deem this inconsequential to everything else and choose to instead prioritize the child that is actively bleeding in front of you.

Clarifying meaning: You can figure out why people are crying and make sure that you can clarify it—if someone walks into the room and sees everyone crying, for example, you can tell that person exactly what is wrong with each child to make them cry.

In other instances, each of these skills can be crucial in settings that are less real-life and more academic. Can you read through a news article and identify any bias? That is an ability earned with the interpretation—you can recognize that the news source you are reading must be biased toward a specific political alignment thanks to the way things are being worded, or through recognizing the author's name and knowing their own personal alignment. Are you able to tell what someone is thinking with a look at their body language? This is interpreting their physical motions and actions into something that is more meaningful to you—you can see that the individual storming at you angrily is likely to be aggressive, while someone who approaches you nervously is likely afraid of asking you for something in the first place. Each of these are ways that your ability to interpret what is happening around you is relevant.

Analysis

The next important skill in critical thinking is analysis. This is the ability to identify the intended and actual relationships between whatever it is that you are observing in the first place.

These observations can be hearing what someone has said, looking at actions, listening to a question and understanding the relevance of asking it, and more.

When you are able to analyze, you are able to understand the undertones of what is happening around you—you can see the meanings behind actions rather than just seeing the actions themselves.

Like interpretation, analysis is comprised of other subskills, such as:

Examining ideas: You are able to look at something that is being presented to you and figure out what is intended by it. For example, you can see that your child is screaming and holding his head that is bleeding, but you are also able to see footsteps on the desk, and a chair pushed over to it that he climbed onto. You can figure out then that there is most likely a relationship between the desk and the fact that your child is crying and bleeding—in fact, you are quite certain that he climbed up, jumped, and got hurt.

Detecting and decoding arguments: When you can detect arguments, you understand what someone means when they talk you through something. You can see when they are supporting their own point that they are trying to make, as well as recognizing that they are simultaneously pointing out the ways in which your own opinion is weak. You can see what the argument they are making is, even if you are listening to them, which means that you can answer them in a way that is logical and rational if you have your own objections over what they have said in the first place.

Analyzing any arguments that are decoded: You can understand the meaning behind the argument that you have pieced together after listening to the other person say—this means that you can understand what they are getting at, even if they are a bit vague. If you hear your child say, for example, "Mama, I cleaned my room, I took care of all the toys, and I made sure that little sister had a toy to play with. Can I please have some tablet time?" you can understand that the argument being made is that your child has done the required chores, tried to help out, and now wants to be rewarded with tablet time in return. Of course, most of the time, analyzing arguments will be a bit more complicated, but in this example, we will start with simple childlike logic to get a solid understanding.

Being able to analyze what is being presented to you can be crucial in real-life instances. You will be able to weigh the pros and cons between two different choices to solve a problem, for example—you can see the argument for both sides, but you are able to analyze and figure out that one solution is clearly superior to the other, and you will go with that one instead. You can use analysis to figure out how best to read a newspaper article to figure out what the true purpose of writing it was. You can identify which claims are being made so you can figure out whether to support or criticize it—a skill that can be critical when you are an adult, especially if you need to figure out a decision to make that has some serious implications or could have some heavyweight to it.

Evaluation

The third skill necessary in critical thinking is evaluation. This is the ability to understand how credibly what is being observed is in the first place. You are able to take in the information presented to you in order to organize it and evaluate that credibility in the first place, determining whether your judgment of the situation is accurate or if the source itself is worthy of being considered in the first place. You are able to understand and assess the validity and soundness of whether something is true, allowing yourself to put weight into what you have interpreted and analyzed or choose to completely disregard it altogether. This skill is crucial when you are an adult—you can figure out what is true or false, what has proper data backing it up or is worth ignoring, or when something is entirely biased and not worth your time.

Evaluation itself is not joined by a specific skill set, but it does have some incredibly important uses on its own. When you are able to evaluate, you can identify how credible a speaker is. You can use your own critical thinking skills to weigh what has been presented to you in this book, for example, to figure out whether it is valid and worthy of credibility, or if you feel like reading will be a waste of your time. You are able to understand this by looking at the representations of what is occurring around you or with what is relevant to the source you are evaluating: You can figure out if the description seems valid or if the opinion or belief is backed up accordingly. You can figure out if what is being said seems legitimate or if it is making up statistics in an attempt to sway your beliefs away from what they may have been.

In being able to judge the credibility, you are able to differentiate between typical forwarding email chains claiming that you will find $100,000 in one week if you forward the email to 10 other people versus a letter from an attorney informing you that the settlement offer you have been waiting for is $100,000. Your evaluation skills will look at all the ways in which the email was presented to you, and you are able to make a valid, informed decision on whether you think it is credible or not. Was the email sent by your attorney, who you have probably been in contact with recently, if you are waiting on a settlement, or was it from a random personal email address you have never heard before? Was the email riddled with spelling mistakes, chat speak, and typos, or was it professional and encrypted to ensure that the email is harder to crack? Looking at everything to judge how valid something is can protect you from being scammed or from having your personal information stolen and used against you later on.

Inference

Next, it is important to learn about inference—this skill is crucial for further critical thinking beyond the first three skills. When you can infer, you are able to accurately identify or get the necessary information needed to figure out a reasonable conclusion. It is your ability to create well-formed, thought-out, and intelligent hypotheses based on relevant and trustworthy information that you have gathered. Beyond that, it is the ability to also consider what the consequences will be based off on the data that you have been presented with—you can figure out what will come next based on the information that you have already gleaned. This is essentially the step of making a hypothesis that you may have been taught in elementary or middle school science classes.

The ability to infer is also joined by several subskills, such as:

Querying evidence: This allows you to question the evidence that you have in front of you, looking for any further and relevant details you may need to make a valid decision and interpretation of whatever it is that you are attempting to judge in the first place.

Conjecturing alternatives: You are able to consider what may happen instead of what you are expecting, recognizing that sometimes, things will not play out exactly as you hope. For example, if you are going to throw a rock at something, you may say that you think that the target may break, but it could also scratch, dent, or be completely undamaged. You can weigh the likelihood of each of those inferences based on your understanding of everything at hand.

Drawing conclusions: You can look at everything that has been presented to you and arrive at a logical conclusion. In building upon all of the previous skills, you will identify the conclusion that seems to make the most sense and determine that to be the most likely outcome, defending it with the information that you have.

As you can see, this particular skill can be incredibly valuable to you. It is useful in understanding the world around you, both as a hard skill in a science field when you are actively experimenting to see what will happen, but also in relationships and interpersonal interactions in which you are able to weigh the most likely outcome of an action that you have chosen to perform. For example, if you are fighting with your wife because you both feel strongly that the other is wrong, you are able to infer the best way to end the situation—you may identify that you are always able to end the argument by bringing home your wife's favorite food and flowers after work and giving her an apology. You are able to infer that this situation will be no different and do exactly that to end the argument.

Explanation

It is nearly impossible to truly have a solid understanding of how something works if you cannot explain it, and that is what makes the explanation portion of critical thinking so important—when you are able to explain yourself well, you can explain coherently exactly why you have done something and how it seemed like the best possible solution. You can allow the other person to effectively see things through your eyes when you have the verbal know-how and technical understanding necessary to walk the other person through your decision. Explanation allows you to both communicate and justify the reasoning that was involved in making your decision, as well as to present that reasoning in a coherent manner that is clear to understand.

This comes with its own subskills, such as:

Describing your method and results: You are able to explain why you have done what you have done in a way that is easily understood by those around you so they can see things from your perspective. They understand why you went step-by-step in the way you did because you can walk them through it. For example, you explain that you thought to buy the ground beef with a slightly higher fat content seemed okay to you in the absence of the type that you were asked to bring because it was so similar.

Justifying what you have done: You can explain exactly why your decisions that you made were right in the first place—you can walk the other person through understanding why you would have wanted to make those decisions and how they seemed like the right ones. You can point out that you chose not to buy a certain extra insurance coverage on your car because you did not see it as worthwhile when your care is already next to worthless due to age, so you figured it would be totaled in nearly any accident, so why pay for extra coverage that would likely never be relevant?

Proposing and defending your explanation clearly: You are able to bring up support for exactly why you made your decision in a way that makes sense. You can tell your child that you are not willing to get them a puppy for Christmas because your child already struggles to even help put away his clothes in the laundry basket instead of leaving a trail of clothing to his room and will never follow through with his chores without being constantly harassed, so you feel like adding a puppy is too much of a responsibility.

Presenting well-reasoned arguments in context: You are able to form your reasons for making the choices that you have in ways that make sense and are logically consistent. You may bring up any supporting evidence first, then explain the contexts of that evidence, and then finally apply that evidence to your argument in a way that makes sense.

For example, you may explain the premises of your argument. For example, if you point out all the ways that your child is not responsible before telling your child that a dog takes responsibility and only children who are responsible get puppies. The logical conclusion then is that your child does not get a puppy because your child is not responsible enough.

This skill, in particular, becomes incredibly useful in activities that require massive attention to detail. This skill, in particular, is relevant in logic and practical reasoning, where attention to detail is critical to figuring out if an argument is actually as rational as it is meant to be. It can be used when working as a lawyer, working in ways that prove whether your client is guilty or not. It can be used to better your communication in relationships with other people, allowing you to clear up any negative implications or misunderstandings with ease.

Self-Regulation

The final skill that is crucial to critical thinking is self-regulation. This skill is the ability to self-consciously monitor your own thought processes and behaviors, as well as how you are using those thoughts and actions in order to get results, allowing for a confirmation or a rejection of one's own inferential judgments. It allows you to question, confirm, justify, or correct your reasoning skills that you were using in earlier steps of the process, or correct anywhere that things went awry in the first place.

Self-regulation comes with two subskills itself:

Self-examination: You are willing to look at yourself to figure out if you are on the right track or if your views are controversial or even wrong. You are able to figure out if there are any self-bias or other negative implications on your reasoning that are making it difficult for your judgment to be considered rational or sound.

Self-correction: You are able to make any corrections for issues that were discovered during your self-examination. If you find that something you have chosen is wrong, you are willing to go through the process to fix it so you can make sure it aligns with the right choice to begin with rather than trying to push harder and try to make sure that your mistakes are somehow justified, even when they should not be.

Overall, when you are able to master self-regulation, you are able to always accurately self-evaluate. You can make sure that you are making decisions that are the right ones rather than the ones that happen to benefit you more than others may. You can make sure that you are fighting the urge to make decisions that are against your own values or are illegal, wrong, or even just logically inconsistent, no matter how convenient they may be, because you know that they are wrong and worthy of being corrected. If you have made a mistake, you seek to make it right—if you are saying something that offends someone else, for example, you are willing to learn, understand why what you said was offensive, and correct from it in the future.

Chapter 3

Types of Intelligent Thinking: Convergent And Divergent Thinking

Convergent Thinking

When you break down the term convergent thinking, you come out with two pieces: convergent can mean a variety of ideas coming together to form one specific conclusion. Thinking is obviously what we have been talking about throughout this entire book.

When you put the terms together, convergent thinking can be defined as a problem-solving technique that enables a variety of different people from different backgrounds and occupations to come to the best conclusion about a clear, well-understood question. This thinking strategy is used to develop a fast, logical answer to a problem. By using convergent thinking, a group can solve problems at a faster pace as long as they can agree on an answer. This train of thought can be considered lacking in creativity, but it is efficient. Therefore, while it has cons, it also has pros. This type of thinking is good for obtaining straightforward facts, such as the sky is blue and the Earth is round.

Convergent thinking is used in any standard IQ test. It is also used when there is only one correct answer to a problem. We can say that math problems will utilize a lot of convergent thinking. These tests evaluate things such as pattern recognition, logical flow of thought, and your capacity to solve problems. Multiple-choice questions are also a way to test convergent thinking.

Divergent Thinking

Divergent thinking is defined as a problem-solving strategy that allows a person to see multiple correct answers to a problem and determine which one will work the best. This type of thought process involves creativity and allows you to look at multiple things at once. You use divergent thinking when you are brainstorming ideas for a paper or freewriting. Through divergence, a person is able to take one idea or statement and branch off to make several different conclusions about that statement. All of these conclusions can be considered correct, and the conclusions will vary depending on the person.

There are 8 elements of divergent thinking:

1. *Complexity*: This is your ability to theorize many different ideas that are multilayered.

2. *Risk-taking*: This is important when considering your ability to set yourself apart from others. Those who venture into the unknown are generally the ones who make new discoveries and find new answers to questions.

3. *Elaboration*: This is taking one idea and building off of it.

For example, Hershey's Chocolate has grown from a simple chocolate bar to several different types of chocolate in different forms which allows for a greater amount of productivity.

4. *Originality*: This is why it is so incredible to see several different people use divergent thinking to come up with an answer to a problem. People will utilize many different trains of thought to come up with new ideas.

5. *Imagination*: This is important in creating new products and developing new ideas. This also will connect to originality.

6. *Flexibility*: Your ability to create varied perceptions and categories. This is how we get several variations of the same thing.

7. *Curiosity*: To create new ideas, you must come up with new questions and inquiries.

8. *Fluency*: The ability to stimulate many ideas to have many different solutions in case one works better than the other.

People who think divergently share traits such as an inability to conform, persistence, curiosity, and readiness to take risks. There are no personality traits associated with those who engage in convergent thinking. This means that all people engage in convergent thinking. There are no tests to determine divergent thinking.

The two different thinking styles can be compared in several different ways. Studies show that divergent thinking and convergent thinking can affect mood. When prompted to use divergent thinking, a positive mood was triggered, increasing productivity. When prompted to use convergent thinking, a negative mood was triggered. Divergent thinkers generally score higher in categories that test word fluency and reading ability.

Divergent thinking is necessary for open-ended problems with even the smallest bit of creativity. Things like sleep deprivation can decrease your ability to think divergently. However, sleep deprivation hardly affects convergent thinking.

Let's look at some examples.

An example of a question that would require convergent thinking would look like this:

Who was the first president of the United States?

1. George Washington

2. Barack Obama

3. Thomas Jefferson

4. Abraham Lincoln

There is only one true answer to this problem – George Washington. This type of problem would not require any critical thinking and is simply asking for a recitation of your memory.

An example of a question that would require divergent thinking would look like this:

Who was the most influential president of the United States?

There is not one right answer to this question. As long as you were able to gather sufficient evidence, you could choose any president that you wanted. This question requires creativity and would call for originality, as long as you weren't copying off of the person next to you. If you chose a president who maybe did not have a great impact, you would be taking a risk that could benefit you in the long run as long as you played your cards right.

So how does this all play into critical thinking?

I said before that convergent thinking does not require any critical thought. This remains true. You would utilize convergent thinking when acquiring information. A good example of a convergent thinker is Sherlock Holmes. He used deductive reasoning to solve a slew of crimes. He was able to take in all of the details of a crime scene and make connections to come to one conclusion and answer the question of who committed the crime. This sums up the description and analysis portion of our critical thinking model.

Once you delve into the evaluation portion of our model, you are making the transition to divergent thinking. Divergent thinking would take the answer of who committed the crime and ask more questions about it. For example, once you figure out who committed the crime, you will want to know why the crime was committed, what crimes could be committed in the future, etc. Through divergent thinking, we can create profiles and answer questions about future crimes which lead to more efficient problem-solving. This is where you will begin to see that critical thinking is more of a cycle than a step-by-step process. You can pick up at any point in the critical thinking process and continue onward around and around.

Chapter 4
How to Make Better Choices:
Logic and Creativity

Every aspect of your life is one in which a singular choice could cause a ripple effect. Whether you make a decision surrounding your personal life or one that deals with a professional side, you'll have to make some tough choices throughout time. Having to make a decision can be one of the scariest things in life, but it is an essential part of our day-to-day living.

We all work for different things that we want for our future, and we have to find methods of strategizing in order to get these types of things. It isn't easy, which is why so many people are struggling. We often think that we couldn't help where we got in life. Sometimes we blame others, outside sources, and general fate for how we have ended up. However, our situation in life is mostly based on small individual choices that can affect the flow of how things unfold.

Your choices are influenced by your basic needs, as exemplified in Maslow's Hierarchy of Needs (Maslow, 1943). This evaluation proposes five levels of basic needs that we have, which have to be fulfilled. His theory proposes that you behave in a certain way based upon your needs. This hierarchy is presented in a pyramid.

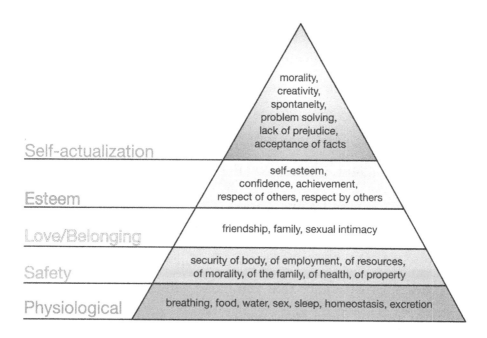

At the very bottom are your basic physiological needs. These are things like food, water, and shelter or clothing. The shelter and clothing are necessary because we have a certain level of warmth that we need to survive. The food and water are also things that if we didn't have, we would literally die.

Next, you need safety and security. These are things like a home with locked doors, a bed we can count on every night, police to call when we are threatened, and other forces that help to make sure we feel protected.

Above this is the need for relationships, to belong and form bonds. These help you get the things that you want, which you cannot provide for yourself. Relationships help bring you to greater truths and give you the chance to learn more about yourself.

Second, to the top are your esteem needs. This is the fulfillment that demands a sense of accomplishment. We all have to feel proud of ourselves and like we have done something. This gives you the chance to feel good with your own character, making life more fulfilling and bringing you to a greater truth.

At the very top is self-actualization. This is when you realize your potential and are able to fulfill this capability. Everything that you desire within this life can supposedly fall into one of these five categories. Every choice that you make will then revolve around fulfilling one of these basic needs. If you want to start making better choices, then consider this hierarchy of needs to determine what it is that you are trying to fulfill. If your decisions have led you to a place where you don't think any of these are being met, then it is time to reevaluate your choices to improve your life. Let's look at a few other methods and strategies to help you make better choices.

How to Combine Logic and Creativity

There are two sides to your brain. One thinks logically, and one thinks more creatively. The logical side will analyze things, and the creative side will pay more attention to coming up with new ideas. Combining both of these gives you a better chance of increasing your motivation. We have to learn how to combine

44

both logic and creativity if we want to make better choices. It can be hard to know how to choose the right things in life, but when we give everything a proper analysis using these methods, it will be easier to know what the best option can be.

Visualization is an important step in combining logic and creativity. This causes you to look ahead. Don't think of things that you hope will happen. Pay close attention to what can happen. What is likely to be the outcome based on things that you already know to be true? What past experience can help you determine the reality of a situation?

Next, determine which side of your brain it is that you are using more frequently. Are you more of a logical person? Do you think of reality, question people's choices and motivations, and dig for deeper truth? Are you more interested in discussing big ideas, new ways of doing things, and interesting innovations? When you can discover which side of your brain you are thinking with, it becomes easier to know what you need to improve on.

You have to start to build your intuition throughout life so that you can better judge a situation as it is presented to you. This intuition is something that we create as we continue to take in information. Intuition means that you know all possible outcomes and that you are accepting of anything that might come your way.

When we think of logic, math, science, and other factually based things, we often forget to be creative in the process. All of these areas crave creativity! How many boring math classes did you have to sit through? But how often do you use math elements now? It happens more frequently than you would have thought sitting in those classes, and life would be a bit simpler if we could easily come up with a percentage in our head, evaluate the loss/profit of a venture, or figure out what the tax on our grocery bill is going to be. Though this might have seemed like such a static subject, you can see through a real application of this information that a little creativity certainly would have helped to make it more interesting in the end.

Don't be afraid of a challenge that's presented to you. If you can't find a solution, then thinking creatively is what you need. When you start to think one way or the other, use the opposite side of your brain for a moment. If you have to come up with a new idea and you notice that you are only thinking of all the creative aspects, ground yourself by exploring the logical parts that need your attention the most. If you are only thinking logically and you can't seem to find a solution, consider the creative aspects that you are looking past.

When trying to make choices, we often stick to one way of thinking. If you have a creative issue, you assume it needs a creative solution. Don't limit yourself with these boundaries. Connect both sides of your brain for optimal results. Widen your knowledge and look at things that aren't so strictly associated with one side or the other.

Discover the beauty of nature. There is so much creativity and logic that occur naturally! Look at the way a tree grows. Logically it grows towards the sun, away from the ground. It develops a large trunk first, and then all the branches, and then the leaves. This is logical. Creatively, we can see how it grows to have these beautiful leaves. It casts gorgeous shadows onto the grass to create weird patterns. Look at all the ways that nature is presenting us with logic and creativity at the same time!

Always give yourself a brainstorming period for new ideas. Sometimes you might feel rushed and needed a solution fast, but even if it's ten minutes, give yourself some time. Go for a walk, take a shower, have a cup of coffee while you listen to some music. Do something to give yourself separation from the situation and the solution that you need to come up with.

All creative aspects and all logical aspects do incorporate each other. Nothing is 100% creative or 100% logical.

There is certainly a weighted side to everything, but you can discover greater truth when you realize how both can work together.

Avoiding Manipulation Tactics

Sometimes, the reason that we struggle to make better choices is that we aren't aware of the way that we might be being persuaded one way or another over this decision. If you are in a group setting and you need to make better choices, you might discover that some people are the ones that have been influencing you. Not everyone has malicious intent with persuasion, but many individuals look out for their best interests first, so you might get forgotten along the way.

If you want to make better choices, you have to start by making sure that you are the one in charge. You should be the person that is able to decide the fate of your future. You shouldn't have to leave it up to someone else! Take control over your future and stop letting other people determine how you might think or act.

Researchers have studied methods of avoiding manipulation, and there are a few important lessons we can take away from these studies (Fransen, Smit, & Verlegh, 2015). You already resist some persuasion, but it's important to become aware of the methods by which you might be falling right into the hands of someone else.

There are usually two methods to avoid manipulation when influence is first detected. The first is to avoid persuasion. This might mean clicking on a news article that talks about the economy, only to stop reading after you discover there are certain biases in the writing.

The second method is to contest it. This would be to argue about the persuasion. Rather than clicking away, you might want to read the whole article then decide to comment or even contact the writer to argue about the things that were discussed.

If you don't even know you are being manipulated, how are you supposed to come up with a strategy? Of course, when we are feeling persuasion, it's easier to stop it as it's happening. It's the sneakier stuff that can make us feel as though our thoughts aren't our own. Again, not everyone knows that they're being persuasive, and they don't always have malice in their hearts. However, they can still sway us, so we have to question their tactics to avoid manipulation.

Start by questioning the intention of the persuasion. Why is it that they might be wanting you to act in a certain way? If you can easily say, "So they don't have to do the work" or "So they can get what they want," it's obvious to see that they're trying to persuade you. If their intentions are for good and they are going to help both of you, then this is a sign that they are trying to do what's best.

Others might use certain manipulation tactics, like painting the situation in one way so that you don't see the negatives. They might invite you to their home turf so that you feel more inclined to agree to what they're proposing. They could end up using other persuasion tools, such as scarcity, to make you feel as though you need to jump on their offer before it's too late.

Understand the biases that many have which they will use to validate their perspectives. Social validation is another method of helping to bolster their attitude. Others might use the example that people agree with them to make their point seem more valid. For example, maybe someone is trying to get you to invest your money into a project. They might say, "Well, I've already gotten several offers from a few different people," as a way to make you feel as though socially, this is the right thing to do.

Check and ensure that your freedom isn't being threatened. If someone is trying to take away one of your basic human rights, then they might be trying to manipulate you. These are things like:

- the right to feel however you do

- the right to develop your own opinion

- the right to make your choices

- the right to object when you feel uncomfortable

- the right to think whatever you want

These are all things that no one should be allowed to take away from you. Empower yourself to stand up and always give yourself a chance to at least state your side. Demand that your opinion is validated among others.

Following Through and Sticking to Your Choice

The hardest part about making some choices is that we don't want to stick to them in the end! Even if it is something as simple as picking what you are going to watch on TV that night. There are some reasons behind why you might be so unsure of yourself even after you've managed to make a decision. The first one is because you lack the confidence to know that your thoughts and feelings are valid. You struggle to believe in your ability to make an intelligent and informed decision.

Confidence is key in making decisions. After you've given yourself the chance to come up with a solution and say "yes" to the answer you've created, then it will be up to you to make sure that you follow through with this decision. Don't back out because you are scared of what will happen. There are some strategies to help you follow through with whatever it is that you are deciding.

First, identify what might have happened that made it so difficult for you to make decisions and to be assured in yourself and your ability to make certain choices. If you grew up in a household where you never had a say in anything and others were always making decisions for you, this is going to play into your ability to feel confident now. If someone always made you feel silly about the decisions that you made, then this is also going to damage the way that you view your intelligence.

Sometimes you might feel frozen, unable to decide which option is best. This can be a fight or flight reaction. Rather than facing the thing that scares you (the decision), your brain decides to flee in order to avoid any mental strain or struggle that you feel in the process.

You have to start to trust yourself. You are the only person that you can 100% depend on for your entire life. Even if you trust someone entirely, they might not be there when you are picking out dinner at the store, choosing which college to go to, or helping you decide how to raise your children. Though others are trustworthy, you still have to trust yourself above all.

One method to help you improve your ability to make decisions is to use positive affirmations. Remind yourself throughout the day, "I can do this." We often say negative affirmations to ourselves like, "I'm not good enough," "Something always has to go wrong," or "Nothing will ever go my way." Instead, replace these with positive affirmations, such as:

· I am capable of anything.

· I have the ability to do this.

· Nothing is going to stop me from getting what I deserve.

· I am smart enough to know what's good for me.

· I am intelligent.

Destroy the belief that you are not good enough, smart enough, and so on. These aren't going to help you improve. Even if you have made terrible decisions and need to do a complete 180-degree change with the direction of your life, positivity is going to do so much better than the negativity that you might be experiencing.

Let others help give you advice, but don't put the decision making on anyone else. When you let others make important decisions for you, you are giving them power and control over your life. Only YOU are in charge of YOU. Forgive yourself for decisions that you made in the past that you might not be as proud of now. The decisions that you made in the past do not have to affect the decisions you make about the future.

Remember that nothing terrible is going to happen if you make the wrong decision. Don't take everything so seriously.

Someone might be better, they might have had a different solution, and maybe they would have overcome a problem that you had better. Stop thinking this way! Even if you do make a wrong decision, you will be able to learn something from this mistake, giving you a better chance to improve next time around. You can never improve if you never try in the first place!

The worst decision that you can make is to make no decision at all.

Chapter 5

Steps and Habits in the Critical Thinking Process

In this chapter, you will learn the key steps used during critical thinking. These steps can be used by anyone regardless of the field or industry he is functioning in. The steps follow a sequence that leads you from understanding your problem to implementing the best solution possible. There are a number of tools that you will learn to use as we move along. One thing you must understand about critical thinking is that it *is* a process. This is the reason why it is so effective. You are supposed to go through a particular process so that you do not end up jumping to biased conclusions and doing something you will regret.

There are six steps that are necessary for the critical thinking process, as shown in the illustration below.

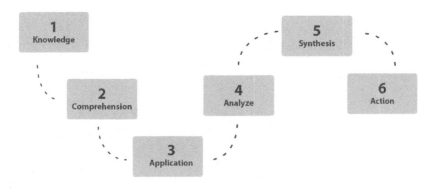

Step One: Knowledge

The first step is to acquire enough information about the problem you are facing. You can achieve this by simply asking a series of open-ended questions. The two most important questions are: "What is the problem I need to address?" and "Why do I need to solve it?" With these two questions, you should be able to generate a clear vision and gain a deeper understanding of how to begin solving your problem.

For example, Company X has been marketing one of its products for a while without much success. Customers are simply not buying the product as expected. By asking the two questions above, we can begin to move toward a solution.

The problem that needs to be addressed is that the product has low market penetration. This is a problem because the company is spending a fortune manufacturing and marketing the product with minimal returns. In other words, they are losing a lot more money than they are making.

I must point out that you must learn how to ask the right questions.

This is because there are instances when you will ask certain questions and realize that there is no actual problem after all. If this happens, then you don't have to proceed to the other critical thinking steps.

Step Two: Comprehension

Once you identify the problem, you then have to start assessing the situation and gathering all the relevant facts about it. Your aim here should be to increase your understanding so that you eliminate any potential blind spots and ultimately make the best decision possible.

There are a lot of research methods that you can use to collect your data. The method you use will depend on how complex the problem is, the type of data you need, and how much time you have available to solve the problem.

From the example above, Company X can use online questionnaires to engage its target market. They can also call retailers who stock their products and get their feedback on the problem.

Step Three: Application

This is somewhat of a continuation of the previous step. You are still trying to get a better understanding of all the information you are receiving. The only difference is that you are now linking every bit of information to the number of resources necessary to solve your problem.

For example, Company X may discover that their product is not user-friendly. This means they must redesign the product and make it easier for consumers to use. They could also realize that their target market considers their product to be a bit pricier than others, and this may require a reduction in price. They may ultimately have to source for cheaper raw materials in the process. Another reason could be that one of their competitors is offering an after-sale service and this is drawing customers away from them.

As you can see, Company X could be facing just one of these scenarios or maybe even all of them. The best way to analyze all these situations is to create *mind maps*. This will help in building a linkage between the main problem, the reason for the problem, and potential solutions.

Step Four: Analyze

By now you have collected some information and built the necessary linkages. This is enough to help you analyze the whole situation from a better perspective. The goal here is to look at every individual situation including its strengths and weaknesses, and the challenges you may face while solving it.

A very effective tool that you can use here is the *cause-effect diagram*. This will help you analyze your problem and the different causes. This tool will also come in handy when it's time to assess the impact of each cause on the main problem.

As you can see, the cause-effect diagram divides the main problem into its causes and then looks at the factors that affect each cause.

Step Five: Synthesis

In the synthesis stage, you have to decide how you are going to solve your problem and the route you will follow to implement the decision. By now you have fully analyzed all the relevant information using the tools at your disposal. If you discover that there are multiple solutions to your problem, then you should rank each solution to find the best one.

To make your work easier, you can use a tool known as *SWOT (Strengths, Weaknesses, Opportunities, Threats) analysis* to identify the strong and weak points of every solution. It will also help you determine the opportunities and potential threats.

From the example of Company X, let's assume that the cause of their problem is pricing. So, now you must determine the best solution to deal with this cause. You can either lower the price or give customers a complimentary item as an add-on to the original product.

Let's use a SWOT analysis on the price reduction option:

a) Strengths

- Increased product sales

- Enhanced reputation with consumers

b) Weaknesses

- Customers may associate low price with poor quality

- Cost of production still stays the same

c) Opportunities

- There is an increasing market for low-priced products

- Sales of other products made by the company may receive a boost

- Customers may shift loyalty to the product and knock off the competition

d) Threats

- Some competitors may follow suit and lower their prices as well, thus making the price drop obsolete.

This is just an example of how you can use the SWOT analysis strategy as part of your critical thinking process.

Step Six: Action

The final step should always be to put your decision into action. In the example of Company X, these action steps can be implemented by a special team or through a specific project. This will obviously require a plan of action to be drawn up to ensure that execution is done smoothly.

These six steps described above form the foundation of critical thinking skills. Whenever you are faced with a problem, you need to avoid making decisions based on emotions or bias and approach it with a critical mind.

This process may be as short as a few minutes or as long as a couple of days, but this will depend on the complexity of the problem.

Evaluation

When you do finish executing your plan, however, it is time to evaluate for effectiveness. While sometimes, this is quite straightforward, such as you know that you were successful when your children were suddenly silent, other times, it will require you to actually dig and make sure that you have, in fact, fixed the problem. You may need further testing, for example, to confirm that the problem is no longer a problem. You may need to have someone look over what you have finished to ensure that it is accurate. You may even have to submit the work and then assume that it will be evaluated before you find out if you did it right in the first place.

If you find that you have failed at any point in time, then it is time to start at the beginning—figure out why you failed and then eliminate your current solution from your list of possibilities. Figure out if the failure can provide you any information other than what not to attempt next time, and if it can provide that information, then use it and do not feel defeated or too beat up— failure happens, but it is a learning experience. You have eliminated a possible solution from your list, and that alone teaches you something! Instead of seeing your failure as a problem, you can use it to learn from as you continue down the process of critical thinking and trying to figure out the problem.

This process will usually continue until a solution is discovered, or you eventually give up, accepting defeat. However, remember that people are seldom really successful in their first attempts toward success in the first place. Think of how many theories are attempted and failed before any are actually deemed appropriate enough to keep—sometimes failure comes hundreds or thousands of times before success appears, and that is okay.

Very few successes come without hurdles or roadblocks—otherwise, everyone would be successful.

Here are the key points of the chapter:

• There are six steps in the critical thinking process. They are Knowledge, Comprehension, Application, Analysis, Synthesis, and Action.

• To start the process, you must ask the right questions. You will need to find out what the problem is and why you need to solve it.

• In the comprehension stage, you can use various research methods such as surveys to gather information.

• In the application stage, you can use a mind map to show you the linkages between the problem, its causes, and potential solutions.

• The analysis stage may require that you use a cause-effect diagram to find the individual causes that are leading up to the main problem.

• In the synthesis stage, you pick the best solution based on a SWOT analysis.

• Taking action may be the final step, but it is also very important to create a plan of action to execute your decision.

Chapter 6
Exercises for Critical Thinking

Time to Think Critically

Critical thinking is a process—not an easy fix. It takes time and thought. Think of the time and thought as an investment in making the right decision.

You may want to write out that process. You might think about it all in your head. Either way, critical thinking involves organizing one's thoughts so that they can be adapted around the facts at hand. It also involves ensuring that they are your thoughts— aligned with facts and logic—rather than assumptions handed down to you. It may sound like a lengthy process, but the more you do it, the easier and more intuitive it will become.

Start by Asking How You Will Make Your Decision

What does "the best car" mean? What would "the right candidate" do? What does "help" mean when you say you want to help a friend? It is important to understand the topic, question, issue, or choice in front of you on your terms. For example, you might want a car that looks nice. You might think a political leader should concentrate on keeping crime down (while another voter might prioritize the environment or another issue).

Ask yourself why you want those things. Would a nice-looking car be there for you to admire it, or to impress other people? Is crime that big of a problem in your community, or is that just something that everyone around you seems to concentrate on?

Before you even begin to make a decision, be honest about what you are looking for as a result of that decision. Along the way, you may even change your mind. Maybe you realize that you don't want to spend as much money on a fancy car just so that other people can admire it. Perhaps you learn that the crime rate is much lower than you thought, but there is another immediate, more pressing issue affecting you. The point is to understand why we do the things we do and to be honest about motives. Critical thinking requires objectivity, even when it comes to ourselves.

Who, and How, Do You Trust Anything?

Now that you have accurately established what is important to you in approaching this issue, you can start gathering the facts. A "fact," in broad terms, is an event or action that is known to have taken place, a thing that is verified as existing in the world, or a piece of information or occurrence that has been verified either through observation, experience, experimentation, or some other evidence-based process. In other words, facts are true according to some verifiable standards.

Whenever you are presented with a piece of information, such as a description of a car's features or of a political candidate's agenda, first consider the tone of the language. Is it overly favorable or unfavorable? Does it present things in neutral terms, or does it use excessively colorful or negative language? Does it stick to descriptive statements, or does it make inferences for you? In other words, is the language there to educate you, or is the language trying to "sell you" something?

Next, consider the source of that information. Is that source speaking from their own experience, or are they just basing off the information they've gathered from elsewhere? Does the source have anything to gain, for example in terms of profit or popularity, Does it come from a well-known source, such as a major political newspaper, or a website you have never heard of? Popular sources can get things wrongs, and lesser-known sources can get the scoop on things before famous ones, but generally, those well-known sources are well-known because they have established a reputation for reliability.

Analyzing Facts and Applying Logic

Hopefully, you will have collected enough facts to help you make a decision. The process of applying facts to the issue at hand is called "analysis." Ensuring that the facts are consistent with each other and drawing conclusions from the involves "logic." Philosophers, mathematicians, psychologists, and other scholars all have vastly sophisticated systems to describe and outline analysis as well as logic. For the purposes of this book, we will stick to less abstract, more "on-the-ground" examples of analysis and logic.

What do the facts tell us in relation to the questions and definitions we raised earlier? What do we now know about the safety of the car we want to purchase or the candidate's plan for decreasing crime? It may not always be a cut and dried answer to those questions. Everything the candidate says may indicate that he is tough on crime. Yet the policies he has enacted in the past indicate the contrary. Based upon how the candidate has acted in the past, and despite his other rhetoric, it is safe to assume he will not be tough on crime. This assumption is an "inference," a logical deduction based on some form of evidence. We will discuss different types of logical reasoning later on in this book.

Note that an assumption based on suitable evidence is very different than an assumption based upon unproven claims, bias, or shoddy evidence. Scientific theories, for example, make use of the best evidence and experimentation possible, but no scientific theory is ever proven to be one-hundred-percent accurate. That would mean the theory has been tested under all possible circumstances accounting for all variables possible in the universe, even the ones we haven't encountered yet! However, "it could be wrong" is not the same thing as "it is wrong." Remember that something with a ninety-percent chance of being true is very different than something with a fifty-percent chance, and the polar opposite of a claim that offers no evidence.

You can never be certain that a source is completely accurate or totally unbiased. Critical thinking involves using the best possible information from the most reliable sources to make a decision or judgment.

Critical Thinking Exercises

Critical thinking is the suspension of your beliefs in order to explore and question topics from a neutral or blank point of view.

It also calls for the ability to differentiate a fact from opinion when evaluating a topic.

Have you ever wanted to analyze and evaluate situations like a master detective? Or even present arguments like a seasoned lawyer yet you are not one? Are you tired of seeming confused and out of place in intellectual forums or in class or in life in general?

Critical thinking is what will help you out of this mess. Critical thinking is a skill, an art and a practice that gets to the core of any subject allowing you to see the bigger picture and challenge and critique whatever comes between the truth and you.

Critical thinking, however, does not come easy. It requires to be developed and practiced before it becomes second to nature to any person. To develop it further, it requires critical thinking exercises and practices.

There are many exercises that can help a person develop critical thinking skills. In this part, we shall discuss a few of them.

Critical Thinking for Students

Exercise 1: Alien tour guide

This exercise is an attempt to get the students to think outside the box.

Assume you have been tasked to conduct a tour for aliens who have visited the Earth and want to understand human life. You are riding in a blimp as you view the scenes and landscape below. You find yourselves passing over a baseball stadium. One of the visiting aliens looks down and is curious about what is going on. You tell him that there is a game going on. Assuming he asks you the following questions, how would you answer him?

- What is a game?

- Why is it only played by males? There are no female players?

- Why do people seem so excited when they watch others play games?

- What is a team?

- Why are there some people on the seats and others on the field?

If you answer these questions comprehensively, it will become clear that we carry around assumptions and values. There are reasons that you support a certain team—maybe it makes you feel like part of a community.

The sense of community in itself is a value that matters to some people and not to others. You may also need to explain to the alien the value of winning and losing.

When you reason like an alien tour guide, you will find yourself thinking deeply into the things we do and value, and you may be shocked if they don't sound logical to them.

Exercise 2: Opinion or fact

Are you always able to differentiate fact from opinion? If you do not learn the difference between facts and opinions, you will only be reading and watching things that enhance assumptions and beliefs that you already have.

In this exercise, try and determine whether the statement sounds like an opinion or a fact and discuss it with a classmate.

- My mom is the only best mom on earth

- My dad is a lot taller than your dad

- My telephone number is hard to memorize

- The deepest part of the ocean is 35,913 feet in depth

- Dogs are better pets than turtles

- Smoking is harmful to your health

- More than 80% of lung cancer cases in the U.S. are as a result of smoking

- When you flatten and pull out a slinky toy, it will stretch to be 88 feet long

- Slinky toys are funny

- One in every 100 American citizens is color blind

- Two out of every 10 Americans are boring

You will realize at the end of the exercise that some statements are easy to judge while others are difficult. If you are able to debate how true some statements are, then they are probably opinions.

Critical Thinking Exercises in the Workplace

One of the fundamental skills a leader or manager must have is critical thinking skills. These skills are essential for problem-solving in the organization, dealing with your employees, dealing with your clients, dealing with your business environment like competitors or even help you when coming up with a new product.

There are several critical thinking exercises that can help improve your critical thinking skills in the workplace.

These include:

Exercise 1: Analyze your competitors

Study your competitors, try and describe their strategies and most important how where and how they make money. Try and discover which are their customer focus groups, how and why they win or lose. Now come back and analyze your own organization based on the same. Identify the opportunities your organization has over the competition and how to use these opportunities to win over them.

Involve your customer care colleagues or your salespeople in the exercise and gain their opinion on the competitor strategies and opportunities.

Analyze every information critically and objectively and find a solution. Maybe your problem was how to increase sales, use the information you have gathered to come up with strategies that will increase sales in your organization.

Exercise 2: Identify and adopt an orphan problem

There are problems in every organization that people do not want to be associated with. Identify such a problem and request for your boss's help in handling it. If it is an issue affecting different departments, you may need to gather a team with members from different departments. Guide the team through analyzing the problem, interview all stakeholders and purpose to develop a solution that is informed. As you do this, you gain visibility as a problem solver and a leader as well as develop your core professional skills.

Powerful Skills Related to Critical Thinking

Critical thinking is centered within the three powerful skills of linking ideas, recognition of incongruences and structural arguments. Each area must be practiced and applied in order to develop to a great critical thinker. These skills for critical thinking are:

- Linking ideas – this is about finding a connection or a relation between unrelated or irrelevant with the relevant or relatable.

- Structuring arguments – putting together the elements or aspects that necessary in creating a relevant, practical sound argument.

- Recognizing incongruences – this is the ability to find inconsistencies or holes in any theory or argument in search of the real truth.

Linking ideas

Exercise: Newspaper link up

Take a days' newspaper, scan through all the articles from news, to sports, to business, etc., write up a list of these articles as a basic concept. Now try to identify ways in which each article could be linked to the other in each section. Identify the overall theme in each section and if possible, link the sections of the newspaper to each other. After this, try and summarize the aim of the newspaper.

Structuring arguments

As you begin this exercise, it is of importance to understand the difference between the premise and the conclusion for any argument.

Premise – it is a statement that has been made before or a proposition from which another statement is referenced or follows as a conclusion. It is the base of an undertaking, theory or argument.

Conclusion – it is the end of an argument, an undertaking or a theory. It is also defined as a judgment or decision reached by reasoning.

Exercise: Recognizing the premise and the conclusion

Search through YouTube or Google some theories, speeches or arguments that have ever been done or given. Take the piece you chose and try and identify the premise of the topic and the conclusion of the topic. It is possible to have several premises, but they must support the conclusion.

Recognizing incongruences

Exercise – Challenging the premise

Pick the same data from the recognizing premise and conclusion activity above, try and figure out if there is a premise that does not support the conclusion. If all premises link to the conclusion, then evaluate the premises themselves and see if there are any fallacies and analyze their validity. Analyze the premises to ensure that there are no statements assumed to be true when they are indeed false.

It is clear that critical thinking is an acquired skill that you can only get if you intentionally purpose to get it. The only sure way of gaining critical thinking skills is through practice. Improving critical thinking skills also requires more practice. Look at every situation that you find yourself in need of applying critical thinking as an exercise and try to find its solution by applying the critical thinking skills.

Chapter 7

How to Get Better at Decision Making

In order to solve difficult problems on a regular basis, you have to know how to make hard decisions. This chapter will cover tips for helping you with your process of decision making. This is a large part of critical thinking in practice.

The First Steps to Better Decision Making:

Stop Delaying: Making a simple choice can be really fun, allowing you to accomplish something and tick it off of your big list of tasks to achieve for the day. But when you come across increased stakes and you have to make a highly important business (or even personal) decision, you may become tempted to delay because It's harder. However, to be a great problem solver, you must not give in to this temptation.

Dedicate Time: Instead of delaying, give yourself a specific chunk during each day to look at the risks, possible outcomes, pros, and cons of the possible decisions you can make. Avoiding thinking about it will not make it go away, instead, it will increase your worry and anxiety and eat up valuable energy that you could be using to come up with more ideas!

Face things Head on: When you encounter a hard decision, commit to facing it head-on, with bravery. The sooner you develop this habit, the easier it will be to keep it going in the future. You'll thank yourself later for bothering to teach yourself this skill.

Shelve your Emotions and Ego:

Making decisions can become nearly impossible when you get too invested personally in the way a choice will affect your feelings and how you look to others. Is there a way to solve the issue objectively? Yes, there is. Just list your options and shelve your ego and emotion for the time being. Think about an example of your business not having enough income to meet your goals or stay afloat. Is it more beneficial to focus on what will go wrong and how stupid you'll look if it goes under, or to look for causes of what's gone wrong? Here are some questions you could ask yourself in that situation:

- Is there an issue with positioning that you don't see?

- Are you pricing your services right?

- Are you marketing correctly?

- What can you do to fix these issues?

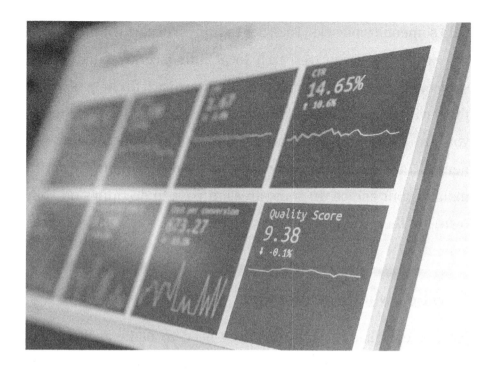

You will always make more logical and beneficial choices when you look to the facts, rather than your own insecurities or fears. Anyone who needs help with their business has a plethora of choices for finding it if they simply remain calm and find those sources. Self-awareness is what makes a truly successful businessperson.

Get Professional Insight:

The choice you are facing, whatever it is, has probably already been faced by someone else. Although you may think of your issue as unique, someone else has probably been through it already! Thankfully, most successful types are approachable and willing to help someone who asks. In order to find an expert willing to help you with your issue, research local influencers related to the subject you require help in and find three to ask for help. Provide them with the facts of the situation, your ideas, and which choices you are trying to decide between. You may find consulting a neutral outside source very helpful in staying objective with making your choice. In some areas, it pays to do things on your own, but there's no harm in asking for advice sometimes.

Question what you Find out:

No one ever has the full data they need to make an informed choice. There are always pieces missing. Even so, it's your personal responsibility to find the right information to the best of your ability. Listening to what your friend says and not considering other sources can get you in trouble, for example. Instead of doing that, use quantitative and qualitative information.

Relevant Sources: Always look to relevant sources for important data. For instance, if you are looking for answers to improve your business, you could look at customer feedback.

No Data is better than Wrong Data: You can use trends in the industry, reports and research, along with expert advice for making strategic business decisions. Most importantly, always remember that no data is better than wrong data.

Always find data you can trust when making important choices, and your decision-making skills have already skyrocketed.

Be Prepared for the Worst:

Another key to quality decision making is being aware of any risks that might come along with your final choices. Ideally, you are prepared even for the worst case scenario.

Consider each Choice: Take some time to consider deeply what the worst possible scenario would look like related to your decision. For instance, if you have to fire someone from the company, what could this lead to the worst possible world? Perhaps they will try to sue or your team will get upset. There are countless ways to deal with each possible risk that may come up, but you have to be ready for them!

Feel Better about your Choice: When you have a realistic view of your potential risks, you can feel better about the decisions you do make. Always remember that people make mistakes, so when you make the wrong choice, don't get too down on yourself. Rather, think about what went wrong, then write about it so you can prevent it from happening again in the future. That way, your mistake wasn't all for nothing.

More Methods for Improving your Skills in Making Decisions:

Our brains rely on mental shortcuts to make choices throughout the day. You might, at times, not have the information you need, or you might only be able to use a small amount of data for making a choice. In other words, you might have to make decisions regularly using only some facts or past experience to guide you.

Pros and Cons of Heuristics: Methods like these are heuristics (mental shortcuts) and are helpful for agility and speed, but make errors more likely. This is necessary to be aware of at all times in decision making.

Staying Realistic: When you stay realistic and know that you, like everyone else, can all victim to mental heuristics and their downfalls, you can stay vigilant, seeking out more data before you make your choice. Remember that everyone deals with this.

The Risks of Ineffective Decision Making and Problem Solving:

Consider a typical business situation. You are confident in giving interviews and picking the best possible choice for a position. You know that you can delegate effectively and explain what your business is about and how the employee should act to contribute to it. In your opinion, you've effectively given them all the tools they need to succeed at work, so why are they having a hard time making decisions, even small ones? Actually, you might start feeling distracted because of your employee's apparent inability to make a good choice. Nothing can get done without choices being made.

Tips for being a better Decision-Maker:

Decision making is at the core of every successful team. This means that your team has to be full of members who can make decisions skillfully and quickly. If your people or you hesitate too much, you can lose money and morale at work. Our modern world is constantly moving faster and faster, making this ever more crucial as time goes on. All of your team has to be capable and clear with the way they make choices while staying true to the policy of the business as a whole. There are always going to be instances, though, where decision making is hard and requires more time than previously imagined. How can you become a better decision-maker, while also helping those around you do the same?

Know Mental Tendencies: Knowing that the mind always has a preference for quick thinking over critical thinking is a good place to start. But you also need to make sure everyone on your team, especially you, have an awareness of the larger picture. Staying with the business example, you would make sure that your team knows your future goals, the reasons for your service or product, and who you're selling to. When you and everyone else are on the same page about the overall grand plan, you will all know how they fit into it and in what ways they can add to the vision.

A Clear Vision of Success: What does success mean to you and how can you share that vision with your group? Clarity of vision is necessary for sound choices to be made. You can take this a step further and keep everyone in the loop with the way the company fits into the world and what it adds to the lives of its customers. Once you give yourself a balanced mindset and outlook, you can work anything out.

A Calm Mindset: A calm mood, especially during difficult times, is the ultimate enabler for effectively making decisions. Once you get good at the skills listed above, you can enjoy less stress at work. When you are overstressed, your thinking ability, motivation, and even memory suffer. Prioritize learning how to stay calm during stressful times and your decision-making abilities will soar as a result. This can mean taking up meditation, going for walks on a frequent basis, or even something as simple as knowing when to take a break at work to de-stress.

When you are a great decision-maker, people respect you more and your life becomes more successful. Tying critical thinking and effective decision making together will make you an unstoppable force in all areas of life.

Chapter 8

Mental Exercises to Develop Your Critical Thinking Skills

Another way you can develop your critical thinking skills is by performing mental exercises on a regular basis. Why? The mind is practically a mental "muscle," and just like your physical muscles, your mind's ability to perform will largely depend on whether or not you subject it to regular and purposeful training. In this chapter, we'll take a look at some of the best mental exercises to perform regularly to make your mind more and more adept at this skill called critical thinking.

Take note that you don't have to perform all of them in one sitting. You only need to do a couple of them regularly, and you can mix it up every now and then. The important thing is you continuously challenge your mind to grow.

Read Books

One way to start becoming a much better critical thinker is to expose yourself to different ideas from different thought leaders. You can watch their videos or read their books. Personally, I believe reading books is a much better option. Why?

It's because, with their ideas written in print, it's much easier to highlight and take notes and revert to them when needed. Plus, you don't need a smartphone or a computer just to be able to access these thought leaders' ideas. With a book, physical or electronic, you can easily go back to ideas you've already read via bookmarks and highlights, and you can also take your time reflecting on them because books don't move, unlike videos.

The best way to read through a book, especially relatively long and thick ones, is the same way you should eat an elephant: one bite at a time. When it comes to reading, make it your goal to read a thought-provoking one from a well-known thought leader such as Simon Sinek, Malcolm Gladwell and Thomas Friedman among others, by reading one chapter daily or for at least 30 minutes every day. That way, it can become an automatic action, i.e., a habit that you'll no longer have to think about doing.

Study Other People

Some of the most beneficial people to study are those that have accomplished the things you're looking to do yourself and business or career competitors if you have any. Why? Studying people who have already accomplished things you're aiming to do will help you cut your learning curve by among other things, helping you see how things can be done or how problems can be addressed from a different perspective. As Albert Einstein once said: No problem can be solved from the same level of consciousness that created it. By studying those who have gone before you, it's possible to achieve a higher level of consciousness or thinking about your most elusive goals.

And what about your competitors? Studying them can also help you see things from a different perspective, that of a defensive one. If they're you're competitors; it means they're a threat to you in terms of business or your career at the office. When you study them, particularly how they think, the way they live their lives, their motivations and their personalities, you can ask yourself better questions concerning how you can avoid being outperformed by them. By getting into their heads and thinking the way they think as best as you can, you can increase your chances of consistently outperforming them and staying on top of your game.

Adopt a Problem

No, I'm not talking about adopting a problem child. I really meant to suggest adopting a problem, i.e., a problem you don't have, but other people do. Now you may be wondering why on earth you should burden yourself with a problem that isn't yours.

Hold on for a minute there, Sparky! What I mean by adopting a problem is this: look for a problem that others are currently encountering and try to analyze that problem to come up with a theoretical solution.

That's it! You don't have to shoulder the burden of solving other people's problems, but you can become even better at critical thinking by analyzing other people's problems that can be applicable to your situation under a different set of circumstances. Another benefit of this exercise is if the time comes you encounter something similar; you already have an idea of how to solve it!

Dear Diary

Alright, that sounds a bit cheesy or childish. Allow me to rephrase it: journal every day. There are several critical thinking benefits you can enjoy from doing so. First, journaling may be considered a keystone habit, i.e., a habit that once changed can lead to changes in other habits without much effort. It's like hitting multiple birds with just one rock.

Another benefit of journaling your daily experiences, thoughts, experiences, successes, and failures is that you start becoming more and more aware of the things that are happening to and around you. Things that impact your ability to succeed or fail in your endeavors. And with increased awareness comes an increased ability to analyze situations and come up with much better solutions.

Lastly, journaling is one of the best ways to process information that you receive and create throughout the day, which is crucial for effective learning and problem-solving. There's something about writing down information and how you think and feel about them on paper or typing them on a digital journal that makes you understand them much better.

Bubble Gum

Yes, bubble gum can help you develop your critical thinking skills! By what mechanism, I don't know exactly. But dig this - research conducted by Kate Morgan and her colleagues that was published in the British Journal of Psychology in 2013 found that chewing gum can help briefly improve memory, focus and concentration. And this isn't the only study that validates the idea that chewing gum helps improve cognitive function - there are many others like it!

Critical thinking requires a great deal of focus and concentration. Since chewing gum helps improve such abilities, however brief, it can help you develop your critical thinking skills. Just stick to sugar-free gums to avoid "crashing down," which is usually the case when consuming sugar-filled foods and drinks.

Play Mind Games

Your mind is like your physical muscles in the sense that if you don't use it regularly, it atrophies or becomes weaker over time.

That's why I'm emphasizing the importance of regularly engaging your mind in mental activities or exercises that will help it get into great shape and stay there.

And what better way to exercise your mind than to have fun while doing it? Some of the best games for developing your critical thinking skills include Sudoku, crossword puzzles, Rubik's Cube and solitaire!

Meditate

Meditation helps your mind rest by allowing it to escape from distractions and helps you develop your critical thinking skills by stimulating:

– Alpha brain waves, which help improve logical thinking, and lets you think about and keep large amounts of information in your mind;

– Theta brain waves, which help enhance your creativity and hastens the rate at which you can solve or address daily challenges; and

– Delta brain waves, which help you achieve dreamless sleep, which is crucial for helping your tired brain rest, recover, and be rejuvenated!

A simple exercise you can do for 10 minutes a day is called the box-breathing technique, which was popularized by bestselling author Mark Divine. Sit comfortably upright with your hands on your lap. Close your eyes. Breath in for 5 seconds, hold it for 5 seconds, exhale through your nose for 5 seconds, and wait for another 5 seconds before repeating the cycle. Do this for 10 minutes every day at the minimum.

Use Parkinson's Law

Parkinson's Law states that a task's perceived importance increases as you lessen the time in which to complete it. The more you perceive a task to be very important, the more you'll be able to focus on what's important and ignore the fluff. When you're able to do that, not only will you be able to finish a task earlier, but you'll do a much better job completing it because you'll be able to focus on only the essential elements of a task.

So how do you use Parkinson's Law to help you learn how to focus better and in the process, develop your critical thinking skills even more? Give yourself shorter deadlines for finishing tasks. If you're given 3 days to submit your report to your boss, give yourself 2 days only. If you have 1 day to finish a blog entry, complete it in half a day. By giving yourself less time, you'll train your brain to work more efficiently and in a more focused manner.

Debates

You can develop your critical thinking skills by joining debates or a debate club. Preparing for a debate alone can give your mind all the workouts it needs to be able to learn how to think more critically. You see, you'll need to see things from your and your opponents' perspectives in order to maximize your chances of winning debates.

If you only consider one perspective or angle, you won't be able to do well, particularly in terms of attacking the arguments of your opponents and defending your own. Joining regular debates helps keep your mind sharp and trained to see all possible angles and loopholes in your and your opponents' arguments, which are all essential components of critical thinking.

Other Non-Mental Stuff

While critical thinking is mostly a matter of training your brain, it doesn't mean it's all about mental stuff. In order for you to develop your critical thinking skills, you'll need to make sure your brain is in great physical health too. And to for that, there are 3 things you'll need to consider.

Diet

No, I'm not talking about crash or fad diets for weight loss. I'm talking about what you eat on a regular basis and how it affects your mental and cognitive performance.

Eating for optimal mental performance and brain health isn't rocket science. You don't have to count calories and stuff. All you need to focus on is meal frequency and types of food.

For meal frequency, it's best to eat smaller, more frequent meals. And by this, I mean eat a small meal every 3 hours, even if you're not yet hungry. Why? This will ensure your blood sugar levels are stable, which will help you feel more energetic, alert, and focused. If you go for too long without eating, say eating only 3 huge meals thrice a day, your blood sugar can drop so low, which can lead to 2 bad things.

One is lethargy and inability to focus. The second thing is binge eating, which can make you feel alive, alert, awake, and enthusiastic for the next few minutes before you start crashing back down to earth when your blood sugar drops.

For types of food, you must stick to natural, whole foods. What are these? These are real food that still resembles their original form of grilled chicken breast, brown rice, salads, fruits, and the like. Avoid processed and high sugar foods. Not only are they bad for your health, but they're also bad for your mental and cognitive performance.

Each of your small meals should be made up of good complex carbs and lean proteins. Good complex carbs that won't destabilize your blood sugar include brown rice, quinoa, green leafy veggies, and sweet potatoes - in moderate amounts only of course.

Sleep

Sleep is another crucial factor that can help you optimize your brain's health, which is one of the foundations for your ability to think critically. There are 2 things you'll need to know about quality sleep: quantity (hours) and quality (depth). Let's take a look at quantity first.

How many hours of sleep do you really need? Is it 8, 7, or 9 hours? Contrary to popular opinion, 8 hours isn't really a rule but more of a guideline - a starting point so to speak. Some people get by with less while some require more. So how do you know how much do you need?

Journal your sleeping experience for the next 7 days, i.e., write down every day what times you slept and woke up, how many hours you slept, and how you generally the day after. On the 8th day, read your journal entries and you'll see a pattern, which will tell you more or less how much sleep you need every night.

The next characteristic of your sleep that you'll need to pay attention to is quality. And by quality, I mean sleep cycles and depth. Let's tackle sleep cycles first.

According to researches conduct by many sleep experts, the average sleep cycle lasts for about 90 minutes give or take. One of the ways to wake up feeling more refreshed is to time your waking up to coincide with the end of a sleep cycle, i.e., 1.5, 3, 4.5, 6, 7.5, or 9 hours after you go to bed. If you wake up in between cycles, your body and mind will be "jerked" into waking up, which will make you feel as if you hadn't slept at all. It can make you feel lethargic and sleepy the whole day. So set your alarm 6, 7.5, or 9 hours after hitting the sack and not in between.

Depth of sleep has to do with brain waves. In this case, your brain needs to register delta waves to get into a deep sleep. Without getting too technical about it, one of the ways you can optimize your brain's ability to get into a deep sleep during the night is playing a delta wave soundtrack in the background as you sleep. This gives your brain a pattern to follow, which is a delta, for achieving deep sleep.

Regular Exercise

Finally, getting regular exercise is one of the best ways to keep your brain in the best possible health. How? The right kind of exercise will not only help you relieve stress but also help your heart and lungs bring much needed nutrients and oxygen to your brain cells. And speaking of the right kind of exercise, what is the best type of exercise for brain health?

Aerobic exercise done at moderate intensity for at least 30 minutes for a minimum of 3 times per week is just what most experts recommend. Aerobic exercises - also called cardiovascular or cardio exercises - are those that train your lungs to get more oxygen into your body and strengthens your heart in order to more efficiently deliver nutrients and oxygen via the blood to all cells in your body, including your brain.

Now let's talk about exercise intensity. It refers to the amount of effort you exert when exercising. There are several ways to estimate the amount of effort you're exerting while exercising but most of them require a doctorate degree to understand and specialized equipment to estimate. Fortunately, there's a very simple but fairly accurate way to determine your exercise intensity. It's called the "talk test." And here's how to use it to determine the intensity level at which you're exercising so you can adjust accordingly if needed.

Exercise for 1 or 2 minutes. Then, try talking as if you're having a conversation with somebody. If you're able to talk normally and with no effort or strain at all as if you're catching up with a long lost pal over coffee, that's mild or light intensity. If you're talking as if you can hardly say anything and you have to literally catch your breath just to stay conscious, you're exercising at a high-intensity level. If you're able to still carry a conversation but with some breathing strain, that's moderate intensity. That's the level you should go for. If your exercise intensity's light, speed up your movement, e.g., run or walk faster. If high intensity, slow it down.

So that's it! Aerobic exercise at moderate intensity for a minimum of 30 minutes straight for at least 3 times weekly. That's all you need for optimal brain health and mental and cognitive performance.

Chapter 9
Powerful Strategies to Improve Critical Thinking

Keep a Journal

Keeping an intellectual journal can also help you to stick to your goal of improving our critical thinking skills. You can write an entry every day in order to keep your entries regular. Each day, write an entry describing a situation that was or is significant to you. Keep track of different problems that you have managed to resolve as a result of critical thinking. You need to have a format that you can follow to address each problem.

Solve a Problem Each Day

Another strategy that can help you to improve your critical thinking skills is attempting to solve at least one problem a day. In other words, when you start each day, you can choose a problem that you will work on in your free time. Then, take some time to look at the problem from a logical point of view by taking note of all of its elements.

Redefine Your Viewpoint

Being open to considering alternative views about a situation can help you to develop more refined and informed opinions. It may be hard to accept the fact that the way that you see things currently might need to be adjusted, but it can help in the long run.

Question the Viewpoints of Others

This strategy is not about being an argumentative person, and challenging people openly, especially in situations where this would be inappropriate. Rather, when you are listening to someone speak, do not always accept that the information that they share is a fact.

Take Out Time

You must invest quality time into perfecting your critical thinking time. This does not mean that you set aside hours each day to think. It does mean that when you have a moment, for example, when stuck in traffic or walking from one place to another, take that time to be more productive with your thinking. As you do this, you will begin to observe certain factors about your thought process and how you arrive at conclusions.

Deal with One Problem at a Time

Critical thinking requires your mind to be clear, so do not clutter it with trying to solve too many problems at the same time. Instead, go through one problem at a time.

Doing this will enable you to clearly state the problem in your mind and understand what type of problem it is.

Change Your Perspective

It is highly likely that you have a way of being and seeing, which is based on your personal and social interactions. From your experiences, you define the way that you understand things.

For normal thinking, this is fine, yet for a critical thinker, this can be very limiting.

You will find that seeing the world from one perspective means that your solutions to problems tend to also follow one pattern.

 Often, this can lead to frustration and negative emotions. Critical thinking needs to be able to redefine how they view the world, so that they have a more open mind.

This will make it possible to find solutions in unlikely places or scenarios.

Always Question Assumptions

It's easy to come to the wrong conclusions by just forgetting to question the assumptions you have already made. Some of the best innovators in the past were the people who just wondered if some of our fundamental human assumptions might be wrong.

Acknowledge the Influence of Groups

Groups have an unwritten and sometimes written code of conduct. Groups expect members to do and not do various things. In fact, some groups take their beliefs very seriously and any member who goes against those beliefs is expelled from the group's fold.

Group thinking is a major hindrance to critical thinking. You must guard against it. You can guard against it by acknowledging the influence of groups. Analyze the group you are in, and determine what actions or behavior the group and its members expect you to conform to because every group requires some measure or level of conformity.

Take A Breath, and Have a Thought

Begin to take even a moment before you answer a question, decide on a course of action, or make a decision. Train yourself to think carefully—even briefly—about what you are doing and why you are doing it. The world and people around us seem to move faster by the day but building critical thought into your everyday life can be revealing as well as productive.

Talk to Yourself

If you find yourself nodding or shaking your head at something said during a conversation or on the news, step back and consider why you made that gesture. What are you agreeing or disagreeing with? Have you always felt that way? When was the last time you thought about the thing you are agreeing or disagreeing with as a topic of consideration—rather than something you simply agree or disagree with?

Practice Asking Critical Questions

When do you think you would receive the best answer to a question? Would it be when you ask a general question, or when you ask a specific question? And when would you expect to receive a serious and helpful answer? Would it be when you ask a question in a serious manner, or when you ask it in a casual manner? If you want to receive the most helpful answer to a question, the manner of asking matters a great deal. It is important that you tailor your questions in a way that is bound to provoke the person you are addressing into giving you relevant answers that are also helpful. Also when you are trying to design questions that will help you during the time of doing research, it is important that you frame those questions in a manner that will lead them to sources relevant to the issue at hand. You are also able to locate relevant material faster.

Get Verifiable Evidence

It is recommended that you get into the habit of learning and supporting your ideas by way of evidence that is verifiable, and also by way of logical thinking.

Ask Questions

You may get lost when you are trying to think critically. You may ask so many questions that you don't even know what questions you asked originally.

It's like the black hole of critical thinking. This can be exhausting and discouraging. But don't stop! Go back to the basic questions and write it all down.

If you write it down, the paper will remember for you.

Be Aware of Your Mental Processes

Self-awareness, self-awareness, self-awareness! Being aware of your own thought process is important, especially since it moves so quickly. Keep those cognitive biases in mind!

Form Your Own Opinions

Even if you are wrong, they can give you a good starting point. This is kind of like the thesis statement of your paper. It helps you decide what you are trying to prove but can be totally different by the time you finish your paper because of the evidence you found.

Do Proper Analysis

It is also a great idea for you to get used to analyzing whatever issue you have before you attempt to make any deductions. Something else you need to do in the same vein is proper reasoning and also proper evaluation of situations and challenges.

Do Reasonable Interpretation

It is important that you learn to interpret issues at length and in depth, as you avoid the urge to embrace information solely at face value.

Confirm Information Veracity

You need to always check the veracity of any information you intend to use, even when you have gotten that information from published books or from the Internet. Even if you are picking information from things you or other people have observed, just check it out for accuracy and credibility. Let us just, in fact, say you need to check the veracity of all information you are considering for use at all times. This helps you to have more accurate information at hand.

Deal with Your Ego

Egocentrism can hinder critical thinking. If you are full of yourself, you will shut your eyes and ears to new ideas or correction s. You will tend to justify your actions, blame others, become defensive or point out the 'deficiencies' of the person trying to correct you. Sometimes, we take our egocentrism too far by associating with people who do not challenge us and avoid people who tend to call us out.

Be innovative

Explore alternatives to seek better and new solutions. You can do this by becoming innovative. Do not be afraid to try. Do not be afraid to take risks. Your mind is a powerful tool that can generate innovation. You must not settle in your comfort zone and be contented with what you already know. Also, do not be contented with what the world and the people around you already know.

Have a Healthy Lifestyle

Now you might wonder why this item appeared in an article about improving your critical thinking. Yes, living a healthy lifestyle is necessary for the mind's improvement. A sound mind must be housed in a sound body. You can never unleash your full potential if your physique is not at its best state of well-being.

Be Creative

Creativity is one thing common among great thinkers and successful people. In the real world, creativity is not the only luxury but a necessity and a survival skill. A critical thinker is a creative person. We all use our creativity in different ways, but we must follow a common process.

Once the process is understood, you can apply it intentionally in any situation needed. It boosts your creativity and efficiency and it also strengthens your initiative.

Know When to Move On

You might be equipped with so much optimism that you always fight for your idea. But if things aren't working out so well, change your strategy. You did not change your decision to reach your destination; you only took a different route leading to it. This is one characteristic very few have. It is called flexibility. People who have this knowledge when their preferences are getting the best of them and are able to re-strategize and change direction. Do not be obsessed with endless possibilities. If you've done a thorough job and things aren't going so well, move on, and still be on target. Having this skill is like having a good map. Now it's up to you to drive your critical mind to your goals.

Diversify

A critical thinker embraces diversity. One of the most powerful skills of a great thinker is the ability to leverage diversity. We are talking here about the diversity of thought or the art and process of leveraging and maximizing different ways of thinking. A critical factor to consider is to always recognize where you are strong and where you are not. If at a certain field you know you are not adept, seek others who are. And exert effort in improving this. Listen to their thoughts and listen to the new directions their thinking can provide. Learn to diversify and be open to others' perspectives.

Have an Open Mind

It is easy to distinguish a close-minded thinker from an open-minded one. A close-minded thinker is not open to discussions and only firmly believes in his or her own set of beliefs and opinions. This is a very unacceptable attitude for one who wants to develop a critical thinking mind. Improving your thinking involves processing new input. A close-minded thinker cannot be convinced or reasoned with. Imagine a glass full of water. It cannot contain new water anymore because it is already full.

Resist Impulsiveness

Impulsive decision making is what we aim to correct in developing our thinking skills. Impulsive decision making often leads to poor and regrettable decisions. When we are under pressure, the temptation arises to make an impulsive decision. Some may reason out that it is better to have a wrong decision than to have no decision at all.

Well, that is rarely true. Indecision is an indication of thinking problems and poor decision-making skills while impulsiveness only accelerates and assures the consequences of poor decisions.

Eliminate Ambiguity

An excellent critical thinker always exercises the power of thought to establish clarity. Ambiguity is a symptom of irrational, incomplete, and sloppy thinking. Now once you experience this state, examine your principles, your knowledge, your promises, and the efficacy of your thinking process. Knowledge is the only weapon you can use to retrieve clarity from confusion and uncertainty.

Be Consistent

Improving your critical thinking is a routine to consistently seek problems in your thinking. Being consistent is a good sign of careful and thorough thinking. A critical thinker always applies consistency and logic in whatever that needs to be considered. Inconsistency is just used to obscure the truth. So if you really want to improve, be consistent.

Practice Empathy

A critical thinker always withholds judgment until he or she is sure that he or she has adequate information. This is called empathy. You should not judge others until you fully understand the whole situation. By practicing empathy, you minimize the risk of making impulsive decisions and half-baked conclusions. On the other hand, once you have adequate information and you have examined it well, do not hesitate to make decisions.

Know Your Learning Style

For learning to be most effective and conducive, know your learning style. This is the learning technique wherein you absorb knowledge the fastest. For example, if you prefer hands-on experience, then engage in it. If you prefer lectures, readings, and discussions, take part in these. If you prefer group experiences, then go out and find a group.

Eliminate Negative Talk

Negative thinking is a self-talk-sub vocal conversation by reinforcing critical judgments and attitudes about you. You convey negative images over and over again. Here are examples of this kind of thinking: I cannot do anything right, I must not trust anyone, I'm not as smart as everyone else, I am ugly, I am not loved, and school is a waste of time. When taken for granted, this kind of thinking will influence your decision making in an undesirable manner. This is a serious thinking problem and thus must be replaced by more positive self-talk and self-esteem.

Have the Passion to Learn

Anything you want to achieve can be easily attained with the burning desire, commitment, and dedication. Passion is the fuel to keep us doing what we must do. With enough passion, you will love your work wholeheartedly since your mind and heart are set to winning your goal. Learning is the key to improving critical thinking.

Improve Listening Skills

Listening is a very vital skill that we often take for granted. When engaging in conversations, what you hear is what you get. You may have probably been in a situation when in the middle of a conversation, you realize that a person asked you a question that you didn't even hear.

Or perhaps you daydream during a classroom discussion. It happens to us all; it indicates our deficiency in this skill. The better you listen; the more information you will obtain. With more information come better decisions.

Always Maintain Perspective

Maintaining a sense of perspective amidst an important matter is a characteristic of a critical thinker. Do not balance in any situation and always view the matter on a larger scale. Ask yourself this question; is it really as critical as it is at the moment?

Check Your Emotions

Emotions affect how you think. Many of us make spur of the moment decisions based on our at-the-time emotions, then end up regretting such decisions when we rationally think about it later. Some of us go a step further and allow negative thinking to bring us down and keep us from making decisions that will change our situation. This should not be the case. You need to check your emotions.

Develop Intellectual Humility

As a critical thinker, you should take pride in your developing critical thinking skills and strive to become a better thinker. However, this should not lead you to think that you are immune to mistakes. If you develop intellectual arrogance, you will be setting yourself up for failure because eventually, your arrogance will cloud your judgment and you will begin thinking that your opinion is the only right one.

Stay Self-Aware of your Thought Processes

The phenomenon of human thought is pretty impressive. However, the automation and speed of it can actually hold us back when we attempt to think in a more critical manner.

Our minds tend to look for shortcuts to figure out what's going on in our world or immediate situation. When we had to fight off animals or hunt to survive, this was beneficial, but now, it can be a hindrance in everyday decision-making situations.

An effective critical thinker already knows about their own cognitive biases along with any possible prejudices that might be influencing their solutions and decisions. We all have biases, and becoming aware of these is what contributes to critical thinking.

Always Make sure you're Thinking for Yourself

People often make the mistake of getting so caught up in reading and research that they forget to form their own ideas. This doesn't mean being arrogant or too confident but just recognizing that in order to answer hard questions, you have to think on your own.

Remember that No one is Perfect

It's impossible for a human being to think critically literally all the time, so remember this and go easy on yourself, especially at first. We all have irrational thoughts sometimes. Critical thinking is a tool, not the default way you should experience life.

Chapter 10
Scientific Method for Credibility and Critical Thinking

The development of critical thinking, no matter how surprising it may seem at first glance, is closely related using a scientific approach or a scientific method.

Critical thinking, as we have said, is the ability of the human mind to analyze statements about the world. And it is the intellectual base of the scientific method. The latter, in turn, can be considered as an extensive and structured way of critical thinking, including hypothesizing, conducting experiments and drawing conclusions.

Critical Thinking

In general, critical thinking can be characterized as an analytical activity aimed at determining the reality of a particular phenomenon. It can be simple, as, for example, to prove to the child the existence of Santa Claus, or it can be difficult, like the attempts of scientists to prove the relativity of space and time. Critical thinking is the moment when the human mind is in opposition to some kind of truth and begins to analyze its basic premises. The American philosopher John Dewey said about critical thinking that this is active and meticulous consideration of faith or the alleged form of knowledge through the prism of the foundations that support them, and the subsequent conclusions.

Hypothesis

Critical thinking produces a hypothesis act. According to the scientific approach, a hypothesis is an initial assumption or theoretical statement about the world, based on questions and observations. When a critical thinker asks a question, the hypothesis becomes the best attempt to answer it by observing the phenomenon. For example, an astrophysicist can question the theory of black holes, based on his observations. He can put forward the opposite hypothesis, saying that black holes generate white light. But this will not be the final conclusion, because the scientific method involves the use of exact forms of verification.

Experimentation

The scientific method uses formal experiments to analyze any of the hypotheses. A rigorous methodology for experimentation is used to collect empirical data, either confirming or contradicting the investigated phenomenon. Controlled variables provide an objective basis for comparison. For example, scientists studying the effects of a drug on the body can provide half of the participants in the experiment with a placebo tablet and the other half with a really effective tool. After that, you can evaluate the effect of real exposure relative to the control group.

Drawing up Conclusions

In a scientific approach, any conclusions are made only after verification and confirmed evidence becomes evidence of a conclusion. But even after that, the conclusions are subject to expert evaluation and are checked until a general consensus is reached. It turns out that the initial act of critical thinking in a scientific method turns into a complex process of checking the validity of a requirement.

The methods of scientific knowledge and research are closely associated with critical thinking, and we cannot deny this fact. It's like two sides of the same coin. But what is this very scientific method? It is very important to illuminate the details of this question because to think like a scientist is to think critically a priori, but to think critically does not mean at all to think like a scientist.

Fundamentals of the Scientific Approach

The scientific method is a complex of methods for obtaining new knowledge and methods for solving problems within the boundaries of any science, however, it is applicable, of course, to a simple philistine life and, of course, to work and training.

The scientific method consists of several components: methods for studying phenomena, systematizing and adjusting new and existing information. Conclusions are made through the principles and rules of reasoning, based on empirical data about something. The main tool for obtaining information is experiments and observations. And in order to explain the observed facts, it is customary to put forward hypotheses and build theories on which models of the studied objects will subsequently be built.

The most important aspect of the scientific method is considered to be objectivity, which excludes the subjective interpretation of the results. No conclusions should be accepted as true, even if their authors are authorities. In order to carry out an independent verification, you need to document observations and provide access to materials and data to other people. Thanks to this, additional confirmations are obtained and the degree of their adequacy is critically evaluated.

The scientific method is divided into two main types with its components - this is a theoretical and empirical scientific method.

Theoretical Scientific Method

The following elements belong to a theoretical scientific method:

• Theories - knowledge systems that differ in a certain predictive power in relation to phenomena. Formulation, development and verification of theories are always based on a scientific method. Testing is usually done through direct experiments, but if this is not possible, theories are checked for predictive power. For example, if the theory indicates previously unnoticed or unknown events, and they are detected during observation, we can talk about the presence of predictive power.

• Hypotheses - guesses, assumptions, unsaid statements. The basis here is corroborating observations. Hypotheses must be confirmed or disproved, passing into the domain of false statements. If the hypothesis is not refuted or proven, it is called an open problem.

• Scientific laws - verbal and / or mathematically formulated statements describing the relationships and relationships of various scientific concepts. Such statements are offered as explanations of facts and are recognized by scientists as facts. If the law is not verified, it is considered a hypothesis.

• Scientific modeling - the study of an object using models and the subsequent projection of the information received on the original. Modeling can be objective, mental, symbolic and computer. New data is always verified experimentally or by collecting additional information.

Empirical Scientific Method

The empirical scientific method also consists of a number of elements:

• Experiments - actions and observations performed to test hypotheses or scientific research for truth or falsity. Experiments are the basis of the empirical method.

• Scientific research - studying the results of experiments and observations, their conceptualization; verification of theories associated with obtaining scientific knowledge. Research can be fundamental and applied.

• Observations - a clear process of perceiving the phenomena of reality, carried out in order to record the results. Significant results can be obtained only by repeated observation. Observation can be direct and indirect.

• Measurements - determination of quantitative indicators of the characteristics of objects using special technical instruments and units of measurement.

The scientific method, whatever it may be and in whatever form it is applied, with a high degree of probability can give a person the most objective information on a subject of interest to him. However, there is one point here that we cannot but mention when it comes to teaching critical thinking and mastering the scientific method.

The fact is that from the standpoint of the scientific approach, true knowledge of something can be true only if the scientific is truly scientific, i.e. it is important to be able to separate true science from pseudoscience (non-science). This problem has been relevant for decades and is called the demarcation of scientific knowledge. For many years it was interested in scientists and thinkers, and now the scientific community has come to the conclusion that the main criterion for demarcation (this is the separation of science from pseudoscience) is the criterion of falsifiability. It was first proposed by the Austrian and British philosopher and sociologist Karl Popper. Its essence is that any scientific knowledge should be falsified, i.e. verifiable and possible to refute through the execution of the above experiments.

We all know that the laws of physics are considered unshakable, and the discipline itself is scientific, like no other. And, on the

130

contrary, if we take psychoanalysis as an example, then many scientists do not attribute it to science at all, even if this direction is extremely serious. And the point is precisely that physics is falsifiable, i.e. can be tested empirically through experiments, and psychoanalysis is not falsified and is more based on assumptions and observations.

When resorting to a scientific method in your life, work or study, you should always keep this in mind, because not only the results that you will receive depend on the falsifiability of the phenomena you are interested in but the approach itself to considering anything at all.

Despite the fact that over the years the scientific method has been repeatedly criticized, its practical benefits are beyond doubt. The methods of scientific knowledge and research are so effective that thanks to only one of them, you can significantly increase personal productivity and maximize your achievements in work, study and everyday life. And in order not to be unfounded, let's briefly list the advantages that a person receives by applying the skills of a scientific approach.

Scientific Approach: Practical Benefits

Many may think that the scientific approach is applicable only to the field of science, and in ordinary life, there will be no sense in it. This is not surprising, but still, I will not agree with this.

Each person perceives the surrounding world individually. People always perceive reality through the prism of their beliefs. But if the beliefs are false and have nothing to do with reality, then actions and deeds will also be wrong.

A scientific approach and critical thinking is the choice of those who can and love to think and understand the structure of things. It is possible to apply them, as has already been noted more than once, to your personal life, professional sphere, study, friendship, banal watching TV and reading books. It all depends on your resourcefulness.

Look around - if you wish, you can find any area that you can make more understandable and clear to yourself using a scientific approach. You simply receive information, systematize it, check it in any way convenient for you, cut off what is wrong, incorrect and ineffective, and move on.

By nurturing critical thinking in ourselves and applying the scientific method in life, we learn to distinguish, as they say, grains from the chaff, to find reliable and real facts behind beautiful words or incomprehensible interpretations that abound in our world. And what benefits these promises in practice, you can easily guess for yourself.

But no less important is the fact that the scientific method makes us wiser and instills one very useful thing in life - the ability and willingness to admit our mistakes and change our beliefs in the presence of good arguments and evidence of our wrongness. The ability to painlessly and effectively resist the manipulations and opinions that someone is trying to impose on us can also be attributed to this.

And one more thing: using a scientific approach, we become able to honestly and honestly answer the questions posed before us, even when this answer is "I don't know." And to find out, we again apply the scientific method, trying to figure out the unknown and coming up with ways to do this.

Critical thinking, coupled with a scientific approach, teaches us to look for answers to questions, instills curiosity in us, gives us the strength to move on and develop. The more often we ask ourselves: "How?", "Why?", "Why?" Etc., the stronger we become as individuals, the more we know, the more serious our arguments will be, the stronger our beliefs and attitudes.

I am sure that now you understand or even more, have come to believe that teaching critical thinking and applying the scientific method will allow you to discard everything superfluous that is currently in your life and achieve unprecedented qualitative changes. However, you may have a reasonable question: "But how do you learn to think like a scientist?" I offer you effective practical recommendations for introducing the scientific method into our lives.

Learn from Mistakes

The first advice involves the absolute honesty of a person before himself, constant self-analysis and gaining experience through trial and error. If you commit a mistake, relax and review it. Do it impartially and mercilessly to yourself. According to the scientific method, any mistake is a chance to learn something new and using this mistake as an example, but in no case is a reason for sadness.

Respect the Person You Are Talking to

This refers to goodwill - a method that comes from rhetoric and logic and is based on the idea that persuasion motivates people to listen to you. However, they will never listen to you if you are obviously unpleasant, unfair, too hasty and pedantic. Your interlocutors will only accept your criticism when you show them that you understand and respect their position exactly as they do, and make fair judgments.

Beware the Phrase "of Course"

The phrase "of course" is like a loud electric car horn. This beep is rhetorical - it indicates the author's use of truism without providing objective evidence of his truth and cause and effect relationships. Such a technique testifies to the author's hope that the addressee of his message will quickly accept his position.

Answer Rhetorical Questions

Similarly to the phrase "of course," rhetorical questions can serve as a substitute for the product of thought. Despite the fact that the meaning of the rhetorical question lies in the obvious answer to it, it's advisable to answer it. For example, if you were asked: "To who to decide what is right and what is not," simply answer: "To me."

Use Time Productively

It is based on Theodore Sturgeon's law, according to which, 90% of everything that surrounds us is nonsense. Yes, this statement can be regarded as an exaggeration, but the point is that you do not need to spend your time on unproductive and meaningless discussions, especially if they are born on the basis of ideology.

Avoid Pseudo Depths

A statement that may seem fair, important, and profound, but achieves these effects due to ambiguity. Strive to express yourself as clearly as possible and apply analytical thinking in your judgments.

Make Assumptions

Nothing can be blindly taken for granted without any attempt to challenge a phenomenon, fact or statement. Show courage and challenge reality. Strive to move away from habitual statements and prejudices, go against conservative thinking, and experiment with various ways to solve problems. And do not forget that you need to verify the truth of your assumptions.

Always Discuss Your Results

One of the most important aspects of the activity of any scientist is a discussion of the results obtained during experiments. By discussing and comprehending them, you will learn not only to achieve higher goals but also increase your personal effectiveness and strengthen your knowledge and skills.

Get Creative

To solve a problem using the scientific method, you need to abandon the type of thinking that contributed to the emergence of this problem. To do this, you can mentally abstract from it and study from the outside. Then give a description of your task so that it can be solved as easily as possible. For example, instead of making your work easier, think about what will allow you to become more efficient and productive. You should not look for simple ways, but you need to learn not to perceive problems as something complicated. Departing from the old way of thinking, in the end, you will come to the skillful use of creative potential and will be able to cope with any tasks easily and calmly.

Attract Allies

Scientists working alone can be counted on the fingers. Even great minds like Hawking, Einstein, Newton and Darwin worked together with other researchers because they were well aware that only support can lead them to truly outstanding results. In teamwork, you will have every chance to test different ways of solving problems and tasks, generate new ideas and put forward assumptions, and get competent feedback. Remember that there are no perfect people, but there are perfect teams.

Ask: "Why?"

Look at the children: comprehending this world, they endlessly ask their parents the questions: "Why is that?", "Why is this?". Scientists act similarly. And if you want to master the scientific method, this should also be your good habit. Finding the best solutions to problems is possible only by asking questions.

Forget Prejudice

To test theories, hypotheses and statements, you need to use an integrated approach. It is able to rid you of the negative and destructive effects of prejudice and stereotypes. It, in turn, is seriously manifested in cases where it is required to resolve personal issues. For example, in order to achieve a decent result at work, even at the very beginning you need to minimize bias and get rid of bias.

Scientists certainly have a special mindset. But this does not mean that the ordinary person cannot master the scientific method. Everything is possible - it is only a matter of desire and practice. Applying this advice, you yourself will not notice how you will learn how to effectively and quickly cope with the difficulties of a household, family, personal or working nature and many others.

Chapter 11

Using Questioning in Critical Thinking

Why do you normally ask questions? Obviously, there are things you want to know and understand with more clarity. Even those questions that you sometimes ask just because you are curious are good. Do you not feel more enlightened after someone has answered your question? You may have satisfied your curiosity now if that is all you were interested in, but sometime later, the information you achieved knowing about out of curiosity becomes handy.

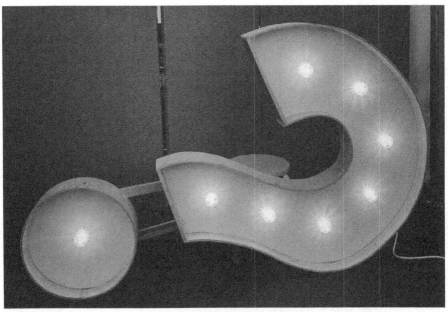

Incidentally, you do not have to ask questions exclusively to other people. You can also pose questions to yourself. For one, directing questions to yourself is one way of exercising your brain, and this, as you have already seen, is great for critical thinking.

General Benefits of Asking Questions

Any time you ask a question:

- You clear any vagueness that may have existed

- You clear any possible confusion

- You automatically find yourself streamlining your thinking

Any time you are considering asking questions in the context of critical thinking, you cannot fail to notice their positive contribution in setting that time's agenda. As you would expect, the response somebody gives you when you ask a question is relevant to the particular situation that you are dealing with.

Your questions actually provide direction to your thinking. In order to invoke critical thinking, it is important that you design your questions in a certain way.

How to Design Questions to Enhance Critical Thinking

- Create questions that help to build your body of knowledge

- Create questions that help you improve your understanding of the given situation

- Create questions that help you in analyzing the data and facts at your disposal.

- Design your questions in such a way as to help you synthesize the information that you have.

So, now you know the kind of questions you are supposed to create. The big question is how do you accomplish this? Simple! There are some dos and don'ts that you can adhere to, and following them will help you in creating the most helpful questions.

Dos and Don'ts in Creating Questions

Ensure the questions you create are not one dimensional

Any idea what one-dimensional questions are? Well, they are those questions that call for a single word answer, either yes or no. Does such a question really provoke anyone's mind to think in a critical way? Surely, it cannot.

Plan your questions in advance

You may wonder what the timing has got to do with critical thinking but, if you pause to consider it, someone making up questions as the questioning session proceeds is unlikely to have helpful questions. The kind of planning referred to in this regard involves preparing your questions early enough so that you do not end up designing questions in a hurry.

Do you know who brought up this issue of serious questioning in the context of critical thinking?

It was an educator called Benjamin Bloom, and the style of questioning he proposed was adopted in the name of *The Bloom Taxonomy*.

There are specific meanings you need to understand in the context of The Bloom Taxonomy, particularly the meaning of Knowledge, of comprehension and also of analysis of issues.

- In this context, knowledge stands for the facts, and you know facts are things you can remember. It also includes any opinions you may hold, and also the ideas you currently have.

- As for comprehension, it is your ability to interpret the information you have in some form of language that you understand well.

- When you speak of synthesizing knowledge and also putting it to use, it means your ability to interpret the information that is in your possession, and then utilizing it in situations that are entirely new.

Generally speaking, you can consider questioning as that critical thinking tool that puts you in a much better position than before; to understand other situations that are similar to that which you have managed to evaluate during your session of critical thinking.

How to Design Appropriate Questions for Critical Thinking

1. Ask questions that court knowledge

You are capable of asking anything you want, aren't you? Yet not everything you ask will earn you a response that is helpful to your critical thinking process. If you want to design questions that will get you responses useful to critical thinking, you need first of all to be sure what you are interested in achieving using the information you get. Do you know how to establish where your interest lies as far as accomplishing a goal is concerned? In order to establish where you are heading with your critical thinking:

- Review the much you know about the situation under scrutiny

- Make an effort of remembering the facts of the situation, and the terminologies relevant in analyzing and understanding the situation

- List all the ideas you know, which you deem relevant

- Note all the answers you may already have regarding the queries you have been having.

After doing these, sort of, preliminaries, you will realize what you will be gathering thereafter is stuff that is relevant to the situation, and very helpful in your critical thinking process. In short, you will not be risking collecting double or duplicate information, or stuff that is of no consequence to the process. Now that you are set to design the questions to use in your critical thinking process, do you know how you ought to frame them so that you can court the best answers?

How to Design Questions to Attract Informative Response

- What do you call this thing or that one?

- In which category does this thing or that one belong?

- Why do you get this response or that reaction after doing this or that?

- How can this or that other occurrence be explained?

- When are the times when this phenomenon or that other phenomenon surface?

Create Questions That Enable Comprehension

It is important that you appreciate the context within which the information you have received has been supplied so that you are able to do your critical thinking in an effective way. It is also important that you are able to put all the information together for analysis so that the information can serve your purpose well. When you get down to it, what you intend to accomplish by your comprehension questions include:

- Organizing ideas, as well as facts that are in your possession, with a view to comparing them

- Translating and also interpreting those ideas and facts in a way that they convey something meaningful

- Giving suitable descriptions to the ideas and facts that you have

- Identifying all ideas that you find are of primary importance, and then you organize and arrange them in what you consider your order of priority.

Do you know the next step you need to take, now that you have finished establishing what you want to achieve or accomplish? Well, it is time to formulate the questions you want to use.

How Best to Tailor Comprehension Questions

- How do you imagine this one idea readily compares with that other idea; or how do some two ideas contrast against each other?

- What possible explanation can you provide for this particular appearance or that other different appearance?

- What are the facts, according to you, that support your position?

- What, really, is the possible evidence that makes you hold the position that you do?

Build questions that help with the actual application of knowledge

Do you, incidentally, know why questions happen to be important in knowledge usage? The reason is that while you may have a lot of knowledge, as long as you do not understand how best to utilize it, the problem you have been facing will still persist.

What you are lacking is the most appropriate technique, which you can employ to have the knowledge you have work for you. It is for this reason that you are required to ask questions that are relevant to the use of the information you have.

Examples regarding how to design questions:

- What possible examples do you think you can give to be solutions for this or that or even that other challenge?

- How do you think you can show that you are comfortable and conversant with this or that?

- In your personal view, what would you say is the best approach whenever you are trying to handle this or even that?

- What, in your thinking, would happen, just supposing things were to turn out one way or the other?

Design questions that are likely to enhance analysis

What is within your reach to help in the critical analysis? Well, you have the mass of knowledge you gathered, and from that, you are going to derive the information you need. Of course, the information you intend to use in critical thinking must have enough credible material to support it. How precisely can you determine which particular material to use in your critical analysis? Remember what you have right now is general information. To be sure about the specific material to use, you need to first break down that mass of information in your possession.

What You Achieve by Breaking down Your General Information

- You are able to identify the motives of the various ideas contained therein, and all else that is involved

- You are able to single out the causes that are entrenched within the massive information that you have

- You will be able to single out inferences

- You will be in a position to identify evidence within that information that you have in your possession

At the time of analyzing information in regard to critical analysis, the way to frame questions is as follows:

- What possible inference do you make at the time of weighing you weigh the different pieces of information?

- What place would you put pieces of information in your possession?

- How can you classify this, that or that other idea?

- When you identify a single concept, would you be in a position to distinguish the actual parts that form it?

Create Queries That Seek to Evaluate

Do you know what you are trying to achieve here? It is to validate the opinion that you will have developed by virtue of the very information you have, and also on the basis of the very technique you have used in the application of that information. This is the stage you are supposed to be passing judgment on what you have observed, and also on what you have experienced during the whole process of critical thinking.

How you can frame evaluation questions:

- How, in your view, should you contrast this particular idea against that other idea?

- Which one of the two, or even more items, do you take to be the best, under these particular circumstances?

- How, do you imagine, you can rate this person's performance against some performance of another person?

- What have you possibly established to be the essence of engaging this particular resource or that other one?

- If someone happened to ask you what you would have preferred earlier, what would you have volunteered as your suggestion

Design Questions That Are Specifically Geared Towards Aiding in Synthesis

What you want to do at this very stage is to try and synthesize all that you have personally observed and done, and then you proceed to develop some solution that is unique to your specific issue. Of course, by now you will have visualized what the general direction is that you intend to go with your decision, and that is after you have consolidated the entire information in your possession. It is also after you have analyzed that information. However, at this juncture, it is important that you be specific regarding the cause of action you plan to take next.

How to design synthesis related queries:

- What do you really think about this specific idea or even that other idea?

- Do you, in any way, envisage having some alternative interpretation of this particular situation?

- Can you, by some chance, envisage a situation where can be another possibility, whereby you can get around this hurdle or that some other one?

An effective critical thinker understands the benefit of being able to ask questions to arrive at a conclusion. When considering the questions to be asked, it is essential to understand that there are no questions too simple or irrelevant as part of the process. For many, there is resistance when it comes to asking questions, as having a questioning mind is often associated with lacking in intelligence or being ignorant. For the critical thinker, there is an understanding, that in asking questions, you are able to create an entire story, step by step, so that you arrive at the best conclusion.

Types of Questions

The types of questions that are asked are also important. The reason being that critical thinkers are trying to get to the heart of an issue, and are therefore not willing to take information simply at face value. This is because these questions will be based on your own thinking processes, so you must be careful to be fair, objective and honest which will enable you to move outside defining perspectives or prejudices. That way, you receive a response that is not biased. The questions you ask should also call for you to move away from your own egocentrism. Critical thinking questions should include: -

Knowledge Questions

These questions are the first ones that you ask when going through the critical thinking process. They are meant to help recollect facts and concepts, as well as allow one to give their opinion of the situation. They include questions that start with what, when, how and why. By the time you have answered these questions, you will be better able to frame your problem and put it into perspective.

Comprehension Questions

These are designed to help you bring forth your understanding of certain ideologies so that you are able to provide information in your own words. Here, you could ask questions that start with - explain in your own words, what is the evidence that, or how would you contrast...? When you do this with information, it makes it possible to see how you understand an issue. If your understanding seems flawed or is not based on fact at this juncture, you can alter it to help you come up with a better solution later.

Application Questions

Application questions are all about being able to apply your existing knowledge and what you have learned to a new scenario or situation. These questions could include - what examples do you have, what could happen if, what methods would you use...? A critical thinker should not be biased, though, there is value on drawing on knowledge that you have.

It makes it easier to break down a problem in a bid to find a solution.

Analysis Questions

These questions are all about identifying what are the causes of a situation by establishing supportive evidence. They call for the division of information into different parts so that questions such as how can you classify or categorize, and identify the various parts can be answered. From the questions on analysis, it becomes possible to identify relationships that are internal. By this juncture, your problem has been disseminated so that you can address one part at a time. This makes it probable to arrive at a well-rounded solution.

Evaluation Questions

These are the questions that make it possible for you to come up with a judgment that is based on certain standards or definitive criteria. The evaluation questions will call for comparisons, making a choice to determine which option would be better and backing up recommendations with information. Here, you are considering different points of view, and working to determine whether your point of view has all the information required for the problem at hand. You will find that getting additional information may help you solve the problem faster.

Synthesis Questions

The synthesis questions bring together all the facts into one solution or find a new way to understand a situation based on all the facts coming together. Through this, the primary solution can be identified, as can a range of other alternative solutions. The type of question that you could ask at this stage would be about alternative solutions or interpretations.

A critical thinker will approach an issue by taking the time to go through each of these questions and then arrive at a solution. This means that the way information is analyzed within the mind is conscious, and there is a strong foundation to support the thoughts.

The Logic Behind Critical Thinking

Critical thinking is a result of logical reasoning, which means that the conclusion of an argument is based on the premise of the argument. This means that a critical thinker is able to rationally evaluate information, and must have the ability to reason with the information presented before them.

For purposes of clarification, here are some examples to consider.

Statement 1

All cheetahs are animals. Some animals hibernate, therefore all cheetahs hibernate.

The following example reveals that following critical thinking without applying logic and questions could lead to a result that is wrong. The result becomes invalid as the argument fails to take into consideration other factors, particularly because the word 'some' is used.

Statement 2

Peter is a human being. All human beings have a brain. Therefore, Peter has a brain.

This is an example of critical thinking, where logic takes center stage. The conclusion that Peter has a brain is based on the premise that he is a human being. With the information available, this makes sense.

Statement 3

Peter is a light sleeper. Peter works at Microsoft Inc. All employees of Microsoft Inc. are light sleepers.In this example, critical thinking has taken place, however, there is no proper application of logic and reasoning to the results. This means that the argument presented is not valid, as the conclusion cannot be a fully truthful reflection of the sleeping patterns of Microsoft employees.Looking at the statements above makes it possible to review critical thinking in relation to logical reasoning and having the right information at hand. A critical thinker will not arrive at a conclusion without properly reviewing the facts and seeking as much information on the problem as possible. You can use logic as the basis of your critical thinking, but before you arrive at the final conclusion, it is imperative that you apply rationale and reasoning. Doing so ensures that you fully embody the process of critical thinking.

Chapter 12

Benefits of Critical Thinking and Why They Matter

How often do you hear the question, "Come down to earth and think critically?" It is likely common to hear from family, students, teachers, and other people who have already seen the world and can agree that the practice of consciously learning about a subject or concept without having feelings or opinions to influence you is the best way to deal with this environment. But is it valid at all times?

The essay attempts to provide you with both the benefits of critical thinking and its drawbacks with a rational answer to these questions. Make confident that in everyday life you can discover the golden mean of using critical thinking skills.

One Side of the Coin. 4 Advantages of Critical Thinking:

- The ability to think logically and rationally;
- The ability to interpret facts objectively;
- The ability to understand the logical connection between ideas;
- The ability to make informed decisions, etc.

Let's find out why it is considered useful for these abilities.

You Are Able to Evaluate Issues without Bias

Most people approach things differently–one depends on their values, perceptions, feelings, or the thoughts of somebody else. All this influences how you deal with one issue or another, especially with such controversial topics as abortion, death penalty, animal testing, or immigration. With solid evidence, there are many questions to be answered. And what's going to help you get it? Yes, critical thinking lets you collect and analyze relevant information and accurately translate it for sound conclusions and solutions.

You Can Foresee How Things Will Turn out

Willpower, intelligence, expertise, inspiration, understanding of the right people, being in the right place, and time is all that makes a person successful in the modern world. And yet, there's another aspect that allows progress to be accomplished–it's the ability to predict what's going to happen and need in the future. How can it be? Analytically and critically, you know the current issues by recognizing the logical connections between ideas and arguments. For example, Heather A. Butler researched 244 participants with her collaborators, Christopher Pentoney, Mabelle P. Bong, to investigate the importance of critical thinking and intellectual to forecasting real-world outcomes. As a consequence, it is known that critical thinking is a better predictor of real-world outcomes than knowledge. So start developing your critical thinking skills right now to know what's going to happen in various important areas–economics, industry, advertising, sales, etc.

You Communicate with Others Sharing Your Ideas Effectively

It is crucial to get a message out to the target audience–be it your boss, peers, or professors–when you analyze a question and forecast the possible outcomes. Critical thinking usually detaches all our thoughts from the public expression of an argument. Only have a realistic view of the situation at hand and how to solve a problem by collaborating with friends or other individuals together. Simultaneously, an open mind for a different view that you can also perceive with the help of recognizing valid logic.

You Are Trusted to Figure Out Solutions to Complex Problems

It is particularly valuable when a person can define, evaluate problems and even systematically predict and solve them rather than by intuition or instinct. You still have to hope for the best– for example, once you have faith in executing complex tasks in a business. In this case, it means that you are guaranteed career promotion. It will also have an overall impact on your life. Indeed, addressing complex issues is a great responsibility. But imagine how many difficult questions you might be able to answer if you put your critical thinking skills into practice.

You Are Highly Appreciated by Employers

If critical thinking is one of your attributes, you have already been demonstrated the opportunities in a professional career. What do students usually do when they graduate from college or university? "Where can I find my dream job?"For students, this is a common question. That's why in critical thinking if you want to excel immediately in a job search, continue to succeed. If an HR expert sees your strong critical thinking skills in resumes, cover letters, or during job interviews, make sure that most of the doors to top business firms are open to you. Many firms search for critical thinkers, communicative, constructive, and innovative career candidates.

The Flip Side to the Coin: 5 Disadvantages of Critical Thinking

Critical thinking is considered as important as breathing in some situations. Like in an interview, or perhaps when you do a test, but not always. In childhood, when you were asked, "What would you like to be?" And you might automatically answer,' I want to be a journalist when I grow up,' or' I dream of becoming an artist,' but then you grew up, and all the innocence and positive outlook were destroyed when life's realities and practicalities crashed against you. Critical thinking is the dream-killer. One minute you'll dream of being the greatest artist of all times, and you'll notice the huge, gaping holes in your plan when you start to analyze it critically. You're going to start having second thoughts and facing endless dilemmas. Are you going to have to move to another city? Have you the ability to become an artist? Are you competitive? The list continues and continues.

You may be proud of your ability to think critically at any stage, but here are some examples that can be detrimental to you.

Your Peers' Jokes Are Not Funny Anymore

It can be a surreal experience to hang out with your friends. But when you analyze everything, all of a sudden, their jokes make no sense to you, and they are no longer funny. How many times have you rolled your eyes at them because you automatically think "amateur hour" when you hear one of their repeated jokes!"And you're just frowning when they want you to smile.

You Care Too Much About Gender Equality

If your girlfriend/boyfriend gushes over that amazing invitation you received to a party to come, and you forget about gender equality. Don't you think you have a little different idea?

You Feel Shame When Your Group Mates Speak

And when, as you would have thought, they are unable to express their thoughts in a reasonable, so intelligent manner, you feel sorry for your group mates and simultaneously feel ashamed that you talk about them this way and that you are like that.

You're alone with your books

Not only do you love novels, your mates will hate, but you can't talk to them about the finer points in the story because they'll probably think you've gone crazy. And they're smiling at you.

You Only Adequate Companion Is You

It's hard to admit, but you can only talk to yourself about really interesting issues. Who can think about climate change's biocultural approach? Who knows why promoting solar energy is important? Who is defending Severus Snape for doing everything he can to protect Harry? Sure, you alone.

Okay, all in all, critical thinking has its benefits and is quite useful in some situations (think about Sherlock Holmes, guys!). But most of the time, it will leach out all the fun and exasperate the mates around you.

Businesses that want to remain competitive and profitable need to recruit critically thinking workers. Hiring a college graduate is not enough. New hires must be knowledgeable, logical, and strong problem-solvers. Strategic and critical thinking is the most needed skill by employers worldwide when evaluating job candidates, according to business surveys. The U.S. Labor Department has listed critical thinking, problem-solving, decision-making, organizational strategy, and risk management as essential workplace skills. Employers demand that recruits have more than textbook knowledge and technical skills, and agree that critical thinking is vital for job performance and career mobility. It was also revealed that critical thinking was considered the most important attribute to help their businesses grow, more than creativity or increased information technology.

Job conditions are increasingly pushing workers into new jobs. Employees can no longer rely on others to make key decisions and are forced to make them alone and quickly. Good decisions include concentrating on the most relevant information, asking the right questions, and believing correctly that too few workers possess these skills. A survey of Human Resource professionals (SHRM) found a total of 70 percent of high school workers are deficient in critical thinking skills. In other recent studies, 45 percent of college graduates made no noticeable improvement in developing critical thinking or reasoning skills during college's first two years.

After four years, 36% made no major gains in critical thinking skills. When these students leave school and enter the workforce, they will be unprepared for working world challenges. When managers say critical thinking skills are highly valued, applicants possessing these qualities will be in demand and difficult to find. Critical skills will become invaluable. The types of jobs and work environments evolve, versatility and adaptability will become essential to meeting real-world conditions and something that practitioners and recruiters need to test for in interviews. Developing critical thinking sets of your existing employees will also become important.

One strategy for management managers is to use pre-hiring planning tests. Individuals who score well on these assessments demonstrate good analytical skills, reasoning, decision-making, and efficiency. They often demonstrate the ability to evaluate the information value presented, are innovative, have better job knowledge, and often move up in your business. There are some tests of managerial and skilled applicants assessing hard skills. Research also shows that higher-level management roles require critical thinking skills and the ability to learn quickly and accurately process information.

Organizations that include both critical thinking and personality tests in hiring practices will have a greater overall candidate perspective than organizations that use personality or critical thinking assessments alone. Helping employees become strategic thinkers can be done by introducing questioning techniques. Better questioning helps to visualize better and synthesize information. By practice, this process can become automatic, with the ultimate goal of transferring information to new situations and scenarios. Some courses teach students to be good listeners, not great thinkers. Passive training does not inherently improve mental or behavioral skills. Active participation in the learning process will be more successful, providing more long-term results.

Knowledge acquired and interpreted by higher-order thought is recalled more than conventional memorization. Knowledge is easier to transfer and implement, leading to better problem-solving. Questioning becomes a vital part of teaching and learning. Perfecting the questioning art begins with establishing what is known, allowing the instructor or mentor to develop new ideas and understandings. Questioning strategies can be used to promote students ' mentality. Create appropriate questions. Perform the strategy. Encourage open dialogue and participation. Generally, open-ended questions lead students to explore and assess more effectively. A professional questioner's most important elements are asking short and concise questions, rephrasing, and extracting more responses from the student's answers. The practice must also master every ability. Offer your audience the opportunity to practice the ideas, skills, behaviors, and behavioral changes resulting from your questions and choose specific activities to enable them to reflect. Think of scenarios to bring your new employee or mentee to a scenario that builds on what they already know. It can be as easy as reading a rule, providing a real-life example of a situation, pointing something on a table or in person. Instead design a problem showing the right thought process. Propose a problem that can be solved collaboratively or through the scenario. Also, use an exploratory interrogation method. What if it were? Explain what just happened? What strategies worked or didn't work? What'd you do next time? What can we suppose? Maybe there's a discussion. What will happen next? Ultimately, provide some feedback or create opportunities for self-assessment. Use this advice to draw on your next lesson and never lose creative thinking. Learners won't want to replicate their actions unless they feel valued. You'll know that when the problem is visualized, higher-order thought can be represented and clarified. The learner will also be able to distinguish between relevant and non-relevant data and will look for reasons why or why something is happening. You will rationalize and clarify why a solution works and see different angles or sides of a problem. Recall capitalizing on real-world situations. This not only helps students use the data in the right reference frame but also helps you solve real-world problems in your company or business. Encourage your learner to think about the methods you're implementing, as this will demonstrate that this is a valuable method to adopt while solving problems over and over. If recruiters and managers start looking for employees with these skills and use the art of questioning for existing employees, critical thinking becomes invaluable for the future success of your organization. Companies hiring and developing critical thinkers have a competitive advantage. With these skills being hired, too few employees have opportunities to develop them in the workplace.

Evaluating Patterns of Thinking

Wisdom is adapting knowledge and experience to a given situation to make sound decisions. It's how we relate our awareness (how we know) and experience (what we've been through) to what we do (acting), what we feel (perception) and how we measure (judging). Wisdom means adding what we've heard. It's studying part-time. Therefore, wisdom comes from (an application). Without doing what we've heard, we can't get understanding. You can't read wisdom; you can't memorize wisdom; you can't repeat wisdom; you can't learn wisdom; you can only gain wisdom by practicing what you've written, memorized, studied and recited. Only by doing can one gain knowledge. Knowledge cannot be gained by silence (idleness); knowledge must be used (applied) before it can be attained.

Wisdom is part of a sequence of events associated with increasing our mental capacity and memory. It is located in the second stage of our human intellectual development; it is amid two other interrelated elements in which one's psychological and intellectual ability cannot be fully explored or utilized. To learn how to receive knowledge, you must first consider how it applies and relies on two other factors complementing it. That refers to the three foundations of intellectual development.

LEARNING: this is the first step towards cognitive and mental development. This is how increasing cognitive or intellectual growth begins; it is described as a deliberate attempt to acquire specific information on a topic or problem. Put data acquisition. Education is collecting, gaining, or learning knowledge or information. Therefore, each learning process results in the collection or acquiring of knowledge or information. All you'll ever get from learning is intelligence, which means information. That is, data is preserved and processed upon finishing the learning process. Therefore, the outcome of any education you go through is to gain knowledge on some topic or problem. Knowledge ownership doesn't necessarily mean you're wise or clever, and it just means you're knowledgeable, and intelligence carrier. As the old saying goes, he who understands and doesn't understand what he does is no different than he who doesn't know or can't. This is why learning (knowledge) alone is not enough to achieve a high level of intellectual and mental ability.

The need for action that gets us to the second stage of our path towards cognitive and mental development; the stage of doing or applying (wisdom).

DOING: this is where the first step of your path towards cognitive and mental development will be triggered. Because learning seeks to gain knowledge or information, the learned knowledge is typically in a dormant state waiting to be triggered. All you have experienced, either through reading, interpretation or experience, is equal to nothing unless it is done or used (applied). The importance of learning is not in gaining facts or expertise, but in its functional utility when applicable in real-time situations and circumstances. This is the source of wisdom, intelligence, and understanding added. To gain wisdom, one must first acquire knowledge or information by reading, only then can one enable what has been learned to receive the wisdom therein.

Wisdom consists in right-applied knowledge or information. Learning something by reading (knowledge) is quite different from knowing something by doing something (wisdom). All acts ' result is different. While it's true you can't have one without the other, and it's equally true that both yield two significantly different results. The do phase is very important to one's psychological and intellectual development because it is the ability to internalize and personalize what has been taught. The doing stage allows you to bring life into what was dormant, making you a creator rather than an information or knowledge holder. As we incorporate what we read, we are smarter as we obtain deeper insight from using the inactive iteration of knowledge or information gained into something more concrete and effective.

This is where knowledge or information is transformed from a dormant (passive) resource into a practical (active) resource. When we learn our goal shouldn't be to know, our goal must also be to use (apply) what we've known. That's how to receive knowledge. Why is knowledge so important to developmentally and intellectually? I cannot attain understanding without wisdom. Thus, in our journey towards mental or intellectual development, we reach the final process; understanding.

UNDERSTANDING: the interpretation of knowledge and experience to gain or grasp its meaning. Knowing is your understanding of the awareness, insight, and facts gained in a practical situation or scenario. It is-rayed through your mindset. To understand better, reading (knowledge) and doing (wisdom) more will broaden your mindset. Understanding comes only when you've done what you've read. In other words, understanding comes only when you have to make use of what you've learned before. That is, only a wise person can achieve knowledge because knowing comes after you have learned.

KNOWLEDGE (learning);

WISDOM (doing);

UNDERSTANDING (interpretation).

Training encourages us to know what to do, experience equips us to do, while learning helps us to perceive and puts into perspective what we have learned and achieved. Knowing is where we view and bring knowledge (what we learned) and understanding (what we did).

Chapter 13

Identify Other People's Arguments and Critically Deal With Fake News

In this chapter, you will learn how to apply some critical thinking strategies to detect and reduce the influence of fake news on your decisions. I think that this would be a valuable skill to develop considering the level of misinformation we are experiencing today. It's getting harder to discern the difference between the truth and an outright lie. On top of that, we have to deal with half-truths, where someone takes the truth and infuses it with falsehood.

Ever since the American presidential election of 2016, we have all become victims of fake news in one way or another. You may not know it, but I'm sure you have come across some fake news. The worst thing about it is that it has become so pervasive that anyone, including a high-ranking government official, can be fooled.

But what exactly is fake news, and can you even learn how to tell real news from the fake?

What Is Fake News?

Fake news refers to news stories that are totally false or contain only half-truths and are transmitted with the sole aim of deliberately causing misinformation. This phenomenon was widely seen during the last US election when proponents of both sides of the political divide began tweeting falsehoods in order to swing the vote in their candidate's favor.

While the majority of people assume that fake news is a recent phenomenon, it is something that also affected people a century ago.

Have you ever heard of Mark Twain? In May of 1897, the renowned American author took a trip to London. While he was there, a rumor began spreading in America that he was extremely ill. Soon enough, the rumor grew from one of illness to a case of death. People started talking about how Mark Twain had passed away.

One journalist, Frank Marshall White, decided to do some digging and was able to contact Mark Twain in London. In a letter to the journalist, Mark Twain explained that the rumors may have been triggered by one of his cousins who had fallen sick a couple of weeks before. Apparently, they both shared the same surname, and when his cousin died, some people assumed that it was the famous author who had passed away.

It is then that Mark Twain sent the journalist a note with the now-famous phrase:

The fake news had spread so much that one local newspaper had even printed an obituary for Mark Twain.

Now that you understand what fake news is, it is also important that I define what fake news is not. The reason is that we are beginning to see more people coming out against real information claiming that it is fake news. You need to learn how to critically identify the difference.

Fake news does not include:

- An article containing information that you do not agree with.

- Articles that are written or published online that take a genuine piece of news and make a satire out of them. These include cartoons or comic strips.

- Any news that is already in the public domain and everyone knows that it's not true.

When using critical thinking to determine whether the news is fake or real, you must always look at the intention of the information. If the intent is to deliberately mislead the public, then it's fake news.

So, What Is the Big Deal?

Why should you care about identifying fake news if it is an issue that has been around for such a long time?

Well, the simple answer is that fake news is beginning to influence every area of society. Some people believe that fake news played a major role in the US election of 2016. Thanks to social media, fake news can also spread like wildfire and put people's lives in danger. In December 2016, a gunman stormed into a Washington D.C pizzeria after it was widely reported that the establishment was being used by a pedophile ring.

It is evident that misinformation can easily shape our opinions. When the news is manipulated to push a certain agenda, as has been happening of late, it can create deep divisions within a nation. Leaders such as former President Obama, who has expressed frustration about how some outlets are manipulating the news, believes that this is a threat to democracy. People's perceptions are easily shaped by information that appears real but actually has no factual basis at all. When the public begins to ignore facts, it becomes easy to label everything as either true or untrue. It's as if nobody wants to think critically anymore.

The internet has also been at the forefront of the spread of fake news. During the divisive 2016 US presidential campaign, social media giants like Facebook, Twitter, and Instagram were used to malign candidates and distort issues. Just recently, indictments were issued in the US for individuals and companies that used social media to spread propaganda about Hillary Clinton so that voters would reject her.

Fake news has the capacity to ruin people's reputation and cause unnecessary distress for individuals as well as organizations. I think I would be right in saying that you do not want to be one of the people responsible for spreading fake information to others or to fall victim to this maelstrom either. In order to avoid this, you need to learn how to take a critical view of every news item you come across.

Combating Fake News in Your Business

Fake news isn't just about politics. Many major and minor brands have been hit hard, and if you consider just how fickle customers can be, you will understand just how vulnerable retail businesses can be. In the business world, fake news is simply a lie that is widely spread about your business and has the potential of causing damage to your brand. These lies may seem minor at first, but if you do not deal with them quickly, they can have major consequences.

Take Starbucks, for example. In August of 2017, rumors started spreading that they were giving deep discounts to undocumented immigrants. This news triggered a huge social media backlash against the company, and even after the company addressed the rumors as being untrue, their brand had already suffered. Some were of the opinion that the rumors were true and Starbucks was simply backpedaling to save face. This kind of fake news must have cost them some customers. Other brands such as Wendy's, Amazon, and Walmart have also been targets of fake news recently.

The reality is that there are many people out there who are irrational. Once they hear a story that fits their preconceptions, they believe it to be true. Even when evidence is presented to the contrary, they do not analyze it critically to determine the truth for themselves. Unfortunately, some of these irrational people happen to be your customers or potential customers.

So what can you do to combat fake news that targets your business? Here are six strategies you need to follow:

1.   Create an action plan – Though you cannot predict when it will happen, you need to be prepared to deal with fake news. Identify potential soft spots for attack and determine your response beforehand. You should also consider retaining a PR firm that knows how to deal with fake-news scenarios.

2.   Always respond immediately – You need to talk to your customers the moment the fake news story breaks. The more time you waste, the more customers you will lose.

3.   Be transparent and honest – You should build your brand around a culture of transparency and openness. If your customers and employees feel that you are always truthful, they are more likely to stick with you when your business is targeted by fake news.

4.   Treat your employees with respect – Customers are used to seeing upper management and large PR firms fighting to protect a company against fake news. But most customers are skeptical. However, if you have low-level employees fighting for

your company's reputation on social media and on the shop floor, customers view it differently. If you have a culture of treating your lower-level employees with respect, they will become your boots on the ground when you need them the most.

5.   Stay calm and present the facts – Do not get angry and begin to engage in a shouting match with your detractors. Focus on deconstructing the falsehoods and presenting evidence to counter the lies. You will sound more believable if you appear calm, clear, intelligent, and respectful.

6.   Consider legal action – If there are people who are negligently smearing your brand, you should consider seeking legal redress for damages caused. It is better to consult a lawyer early on rather than waiting until later when things get out of hand.

Fake news that targets your business can really cause a lot of damage to your bottom line. Just remember to be persistent in presenting the actual facts and do not fall into the trap of people spreading lies. Their goal is to cost you revenue, get you to give up, and shut your business down. Keep talking to your customers and don't stop trying to win their loyalty back.

Identifying Fake News

Here are some useful tips on how to read your news critically:

1. Scrutinize the source of the news – You need to be very careful when you see a story that is from an unknown source. Investigate the source's website and search for more information. Though it is not always the case, most of the stories carried by national and international news organizations are reliable and have been verified. Learn to check the URL of the website to see if the news organization is genuine.

2. Dig deeper - If an article mentions its sources, dig deeper to find out who those sources are and whether they are credible. If the article doesn't mention any sources or quotes a 'friend' or anonymous 'expert', you shouldn't trust the information.

3. Confirm from other news sources – If a news piece is genuine, then it is highly likely that there will be other reliable sources that will carry the story. If other reliable news outlets don't have the story, then you need to be wary of it.

Sometimes critical thinking requires you to stop for a minute and think logically. You need to learn how to apply reason and logic when reading and thinking about the news. This is very important, especially if you plan on clicking the 'Share' button.

From a practical perspective, you need to develop an attitude of constantly asking questions. Why did the person write the article? What was their motive? What does the author want you to think, feel, or do after reading it?

Fake news is meant to manipulate you, and the only way to find out the truth is through critical thinking. By developing your critical thinking skills, you will become immune to manipulation and be able to see truths that were previously hidden.

Here are the key points of the chapter:

•   Fake news refers to news stories that are false and meant to deliberately cause misinformation.

•   Fake news does not include information you disagree with, satirical news content, or information that everybody already knows to be false.

•   To combat fake news that targets your business, you have to create an action plan in advance, respond quickly, transparently, and honestly, and always treat your employees with respect. Calmly present the facts and seek legal counsel, if necessary.

•   To spot fake news, you need to investigate the source, dig deeper, and confirm from other reliable news sources.

•   Adopting a critical thinking approach when reading the news is the best way to avoid being manipulated by fake news.

• Always ask why the author wrote the article and what they want people to do after reading it.

Conclusion

If you have gone through the proper process of understanding the problem, looking at all possible options, gathering information for the solutions, and evaluating everything, you should rest assured that you should be able to stand alone in the decision you are going to make. You're putting your critical thinking skills into practice by going through this whole process. As with other things that are done for the very first time, it may seem unorthodox, but as you continue to practice these techniques, your critical thinking skills will grow and evolve more.

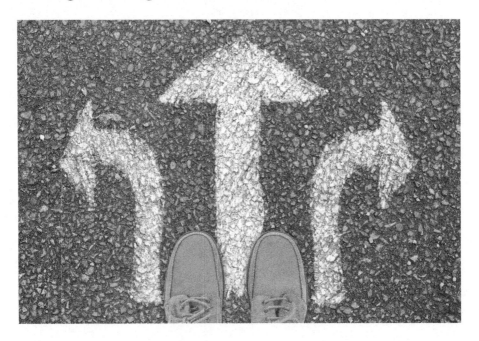

You need to understand that, generally speaking, the ability to think critically varies from person to person based on their level of exposure to the different issues and how well they managed to solve them. The good thing is that you can learn and develop the ability to think critically and make the most of it.

Critical thinking sounds harder than it is. And just like everything else, a lot of people try to make it more complicated so they can benefit. Everyone is seeking an advantage in this relatively simple game of life. There's no reason to let them have one. Always remember to *Simplify*. There is absolutely nothing out there that cannot be reduced to simple terms. Even critical thinking.

In most of your encounters each day, stupidity is encouraged so people can get your money. But sometimes they just want to control you, or build up their own ego. Whatever the motives, the rest of the world tries very hard to make you think stupidly.

Accept Rejection – No matter how hard you try, you cannot please everyone. Therefore, you will go through times when you are rejected, whether it is in personal relationships, the workplace or society at large. Do not give rejection the power to delve you into negative thinking. Instead, accept rejection and always look for the opportunity that comes from it.

Be Solution Oriented – You will face problems at some point even when you have positive energy all the time. To remain with positive energy, you should think about the solutions to the problems, rather than the devastation of the problems. You will find that with time, you are always able to make things better.

Stay Present – Once you are facing an issue, make sure that you focus on the problem in the present, instead of using your energy thinking about the problem in the future, or bringing up incidences from the past. Losing focus makes it difficult to remain positive, and also brings up conflicting emotions that feed negativity. By being present, you can find a positive solution to a specific problem.

Put Yourself First – Positive thinking extends beyond your mind and also affect you physically and mentally. In order to habitually think positively, you must take care of your body and your mind. This means that you stay in shape, get rest when it is necessary, and live a healthy lifestyle. These actions ensure that you live without experiencing stress or anxiety.

The more stupid we are, the more it costs us. Time, anxiety, cash, and frequently pain and suffering too. And Stupidity is BIG business. Everywhere we are stupid, someone else is collecting the cash. Start using your skills.

Made in the USA
Las Vegas, NV
12 December 2023

82590998R10105